ART-TYPE EDITION

LINCOLN'S STORIES and SPEECHES

Edited by

EDWARD FRANK ALLEN

THE WORLD'S POPULAR CLASSICS

BOOKS, INC.
PUBLISHERS
NEW YORK

PRINTED IN THE UNITED STATES OF AMERICA

LINCOLN'S STORIES AND SPEECHES

A BIOGRAPHICAL SKETCH OF ABRAHAM LINCOLN

I

Abraham Lincoln was not only a great American, but he was a man of outstanding personality. He was a simple man, a genial man, a human man, and an honest man. These characteristics, coupled with his rugged genius, add up to greatness.

On December 20, 1859, he wrote a letter to his friend Jesse W. Fell, of Bloomington, Ill., telling something of his life and the history of his family. This was the year before his election to the Presidency, and the letter shows that he was not anxious to cover up his humble background. Here is the letter:

"I was born, February 12, 1809, in Hardin County, Kentucky. My parents were both born in Virginia, of undistinguished families—second families, perhaps I should say. My mother, who died in my tenth year, was of a family of the name of Hanks, some of whom now reside in Adams and others in Macon County, Illinois. My paternal grandfather, Abraham Lincoln, emigrated from Rockingham County, Virginia, to Kentucky, about 1781 or 1782, where, a year or two later, he was killed by Indians, not in battle, but by stealth, when he was laboring to open a farm in the forest. His ancestors, who were Quakers, went to Virginia from Berks County, Pennsylvania. An effort to identify them with the New England family of the same name ended in nothing more than a similarity of Christian names in both families, such as Enoch, Levi, Mordecai, Solomon, Abraham, and the like.

"My father, at the death of his father, was but six years of age, and he grew up literally without education. He removed from Kentucky to what is now Spencer County, Indiana, in my eighth year. We reached our new home about the time the State came into the Union (1816). It was a wild region, with many bears and other wild animals still in the woods. There I grew up. There were some schools, so-called, but no qualification was ever required of a teacher beyond 'readin', writin', and cipherin' ' to the Rule of Three. If a straggler, supposed to understand Latin, happened to sojourn in the neighborhood, he was looked upon as a wizard. There was absolutely nothing to excite ambition for education. Of course, when I came of age, I did not know much. Still, somehow, I could read, write, and cipher to the Rule of Three, but that was all. I have not been to school since. The little advance I now have upon this store of education I have picked up from time to time under the pressure of necessity.

"I was raised to farm-work, which I continued until I was twenty-two. At twenty-one I came to Illinois and passed the first year in Macon County. Then I got to New Salem, at that time in Sangamon, now in Menard County, where I remained a year as a sort of clerk in a store. Then came the Black Hawk War, and I was elected a captain of volunteers—a success which gave me more pleasure than any I have had since. I went through the campaign, was elated, ran for the Legislature in the same year (1832), and was beaten—the only time I have ever been beaten by the people. The next, and three succeeding biennial elections, I was elected to the Legislature. I was not a candidate afterwards. During this legislative period, I had studied law and removed to Springfield to practice it. In 1846 I was once elected to the lower House of Congress, but was not a candidate for re-election. From 1849 to 1854, both inclusive, practiced law more assiduously than ever before. Always a Whig in politics, and generally on the Whig electoral ticket making active canvasses. I was losing interest in politics when the repeal of the Missouri Compromise aroused me again. What I have done since then is pretty well known.

"If any personal description of me is thought desirable, it may be said, I am, in height, six feet four inches, nearly; lean in flesh, weighing, on an average, one hundred and eighty pounds; dark complexion, with coarse black hair, and gray eyes. No other marks or brands recollected.

"Yours truly,

"A. Lincoln."

Lincoln wrote another sketch of his life for campaign purposes in 1860, and from these notes and later research by his biographers, supplemented by voluminous historical records, his life story has been adequately presented.

His ancestor Samuel Lincoln came from England in 1637 and settled in Salem, Mass. Samuel was the progenitor of some other distinguished Americans, including army generals and state governors, in Revolutionary days.

Abraham Lincoln's grandfather settled in Kentucky in about the year 1781. Three years later he was killed by Indians, leaving six-year-old Thomas, who was to father a great and noble President of the United States.

It is on record that Thomas Lincoln married Nancy Hanks in Washington County, Kentucky, on June 12, 1806. Abraham was the second child of this marriage.

(A younger son had died in infancy.) His early life was spent amid the humble surroundings of a pioneer's family, but not in squalor as some biographers have led us to believe. The boy was about eight years old when his parents moved to Indiana, where for a time the family lived in a rude cabin built of logs, one side of which was open to provide the combined functions of door and windows.

From this home the boy went to school, but Lincoln himself says that the entire amount of his schooling did not total a full year. He was an unusually apt pupil, however, and made better progress than any of his schoolmates. At night in the Lincoln cabin he would study by the light of spicewood brushes braced against a log in the fireplace.

After two years in Indiana, Abraham's mother died and his father a year later, married a Mrs. Sarah Johnston. As a stepmother she proved a complete success, and a lifelong friendship developed between her and Lincoln.

At the age of seventeen Lincoln, as a ferryman, earned his first dollar by rowing two travelers and their baggage to a passing steamboat in the Ohio River. Two years later he took his first trip to New Orleans as a hired hand on a flatboat. His pay was eight dollars a month and his passage home. There was at least one exciting incident on the voyage, for one night while the boat was tied to the shore of the Mississippi River it was attacked by a gang of desperate Negroes, and several of the crew were wounded in the fight that ensued.

It was in 1830 that the Lincolns moved to Illinois, the State that was to be so proud of the fact in later years, and settled on the banks of the Sangamon River. Here, in helping his father to establish a farm, he split rails for the fences that divided their land. Here also with two other young men he built a flatboat for a neighbor whom he accompanied on it to New Orleans. On this second trip to the "Crescent City" he saw for the first time the vicious side of slavery—Negroes in chains, intimidated, torn from their loved ones, whipped, sold into bondage.

He was shocked at the brutality of it all, and his sense of compassion and justice was seething in revolt. Deeply moved, he said to his friends:

"Boys, let's get away from this. If ever I get a chance to hit that thing [he meant the institution of slavery], I'll hit it hard."

Mr. Lincoln had some distance to go before he could strike a blow at slavery. He got a job as a clerk in a store at New Salem and in his spare time he began to educate himself with the sympathetic help of the village schoolteacher. Later he studied surveying.

A year after he came to New Salem the Black Hawk War broke out, and he enlisted. He was elected captain of his company and demonstrated his qualities of leadership. When his company was disbanded he re-enlisted as a private, but though he remained in service three months, he did not participate in any battle.

When he returned from the Black Hawk War, Lincoln entered business as a storekeeper, in addition to which for a time he was postmaster. Within a year, however, he and his partner sold out their business, receiving payment in promises. The buyers within a short time failed, and they left for other parts. Until his retirement from Congress in 1849 Lincoln bore the burden of the debt he had incurred by this deal.

2

Lincoln began his political career in 1832 as a candidate for Representative in the General Assembly from Sangamon County. His opponent was elected, and Lincoln sustained his only defeat in running for an office that was filled by the voice of the people. He was then twenty-four years old. His manners were unpolished and his clothes looked as if he had slept in them, but he won the respect and confidence of all with whom he came in contact. He had rare common sense and unimpeachable honesty plus a sense of humor that appealed to everyone. He was good company, and his droll stories—most of which pointed a moral with telling effect—are quoted and laughed at today. Yet his friends said that he never drank spirituous liquors, and that, in those days, he never even used tobacco.

Again he became a candidate for the Legislature in 1834, and this time he was elected. A colleague induced him to begin the study of law and lent him books. He was re-elected to the Legislature in 1836 with the largest vote cast for any candidate on the legislative ticket from Sangamon County. His popularity was growing.

This Legislature was outstanding for the number of its members who became distinguished later in State or National history. Among these was Stephen A. Douglas, who became United States Senator in 1847 and debated publicly with Lincoln in a subsequent senatorial campaign.

When he returned from the Legislature of 1836-37, Lincoln began to practice law in partnership with John T. Stuart. Lincoln's friend Joshua F. Speed, a Springfield storekeeper, tells of Lincoln's acceptance of his invitation to share his room.

"He had ridden into town on a borrowed horse, and engaged from the only cabinetmaker in the village a single bedstead. He came into my store, set his saddle-bags on the counter, and inquired what the furniture for a single bedstead would cost. I took slate and pencil, made a calculation, and found the sum for furniture, complete, would amount to seventeen dollars in all. Said he: 'It is probably cheap enough; but I want to say that, cheap as it is, I have not the money to pay. But if you will credit me until Christmas, and my experiment as a lawyer here is a success, I will pay you then. If I fail in that, I will probably never pay you at all.' The tone of his voice was so melancholy that I felt for him. I looked at him, and I thought then, as I think now, that I never saw so gloomy and melancholy a face in my life. I said to him, 'So small a debt seems to affect you so deeply, I think I can suggest a plan by which you will be able to attain your end without any debt. I have a very large room, and a very large double-bed in it, which you are perfectly welcome to share with me if you choose.' 'Where is your room?' he asked. 'Upstairs,' said I, pointing to the stairs leading from the store to my room. Without saying a word, he took his saddle-bags on his arm, went upstairs, set them down on the floor, came down again, and, with a face beaming with pleasure and smiles, exclaimed, 'Well, Speed, I'm moved.' "

Later he became a law partner of Judge Stephen T. Logan and after that, of William H. Herndon, which partnership continued, nominally at least, until his death. He enjoyed his life as a lawyer, for during this period he made lifelong friendships.

One of his earliest public utterances on the subject of slavery was in an address before the Young Men's Lyceum at Springfield, Illinois, in January, 1837. There had been mob outrages and lynchings in some of the Southern States, and in St. Louis a Negro charged with murder had been burned. In his speech he said:

"There is no grievance that is a fit object of redress by mob law. In any case that may arise, as, for instance, the promulgation of abolitionism, one of two positions is necessarily true—that the thing is right within itself, and therefore deserves protection of all law and all good citizens; or it is wrong, and, therefore, proper to be prohibited by legal enactments; and in neither case is the interposition of mob law either necessary, justifiable, or excusable."

During the legislative session in March of the same year he protested vigorously against a series of proslavery resolutions that had been adopted by that body.

Mr. Lincoln married Miss Mary Todd on November 4, 1842. In 1846 he was elected as Representative in Congress from the Springfield district. He opposed the administration's position with regard to the Mexican War, and supported a bill for the abolition of slavery in the District of Columbia, "with the consent of the voters of the District and with compensation to the owners."

3

In 1849 Mr. Lincoln retired from Congress, and during the following five years, urged by the necessity of providing for his family, he practiced his profession of law. He was called again into the political arena in 1854 by the passage of the Kansas-Nebraska Bill, which repealed the Missouri Compromise and paved the way for the admission of slavery into free territory. Lincoln became a leader of the opposition to that measure.

Between 1856 and 1858 Lincoln did not give much time to politics. Instead, for the most part, he devoted his attention to the practice of law. But at the State Convention of the Republicans on June 16 of the latter year a resolution was adopted announcing Abraham Lincoln as its "first and only choice for United States Senator to fill the vacancy about to be created by the expiration of Mr. Douglas' term of office."

Lincoln's response to this resolution was one of the most important utterances of his life. The part that is best remembered is the following:

"A house divided against itself cannot stand. I believe this Government cannot endure permanently half slave and half free. I do not expect the Union to be dissolved —I do not expect the house to fall—but I do expect it will cease to be divided. It will become all one thing or all the other. Either the opponents of slavery will arrest the further spread of it, and place it where the public mind shall rest in the belief that it is in course of ultimate extinction; or its advocates will push it forward, till it shall become alike lawful in all the States—old as well as new, North as well as South."

He closed his speech with the ringing words: "The result is not doubtful. We shall not fail—if we stand firm, we shall not fail. Wise counsels may accelerate or mistakes delay it, but sooner or later the victory is sure to come."

A few months later Lincoln challenged Senator Douglas to a series of debates that attracted the attention of the entire country. The showing made by Douglas lost him his former support in the slave States and helped to defeat him when he ran for the Presidency in 1860. Further speeches contributed to Lincoln's popularity, and when the National Republican Convention met at Chicago, May 16, 1860, he was unanimously nominated on the final ballot amid wild enthusiasm. The runner-up was William H. Seward, whom Lincoln later appointed Secretary of State in his cabinet.

The campaign was marked by extraordinary bitterness on the part of opposition, particularly in the South. They called him ignorant and uncouth; pictured him as a baboon; described him as a rum-soaked drunkard, in spite of his absolutely abstemious habits. From ten of the Southern States not a single vote for him was returned. But he was elected with a plurality of the popular vote and 180 electoral votes out of a possible 303.

4

When, on the morning of February 11, 1861, he left his home at Springfield, Illinois, to take up the duties of President at Washington, he stood on the back platform of the train and said to his friends and neighbors who had come to see him off:

"My Friends: No one not in my position can realize the sadness I feel at this parting. To this people I owe all that I am. Here I have lived more than a quarter of a century. Here my children were born, and here one of them lies buried. I know not how soon I shall see you again. I go to assume a task more difficult than that which has devolved upon any other man since the days of Washington. He never would have succeeded except for the aid of Divine Providence, upon which he at all times relied. I feel that I cannot succeed without the same divine blessing which sustained him; and on the same Almighty Being I place my reliance for support. And I hope you, my friends, will all pray that I may receive that divine assistance, without which I cannot succeed, but with which success is certain. Again, I bid you an affectionate farewell."

There was a plot to assassinate Lincoln in Baltimore, but it was discovered in time to re-route his train. In the company of Allan Pinkerton, the detective, he arrived safely in Washington the morning of February 23.

The rest is history. . . . The inauguration, with the National capital in ferment, seething with Secessionists and Unionists. . . . Then four years of fratricidal strife, the Civil War that stooped Lincoln's shoulders with care and bowed his head with grief. . . . From the fall of Fort Sumter to the battle of Gettysburg, though his patience and his faith were sorely tried, Lincoln never lost confidence in the Union cause.

When he issued his Emancipation Proclamation that freed the Negro slaves, he recommended compensation for their owners. This would have prevented much hatred and bloodshed. He was re-elected in 1864, and on

April 9 of the following year Lee surrendered to Grant.

Five days later the Nation was plunged into gloom when the president was shot and killed by the assassin John Wilkes Booth. National rejoicing over the ending of bloodshed turned to National sorrow at the sudden passing of a great and good man.

Today Lincoln remains as a symbol of the finest type of Americanism. Other Presidents still awaken reverence, but among the immortal figures of our country Lincoln stands out because we not only revere him—we love him. The closing paragraph of his second inaugural address is an index of his character, his compassion:

"With malice toward none; with charity for all; with firmness in the right, as God gives us to see the right, let us strive on to finish the work that we are in; to bind up the nation's wounds; to care for him who shall have borne the battle, and for his widow and his orphan—to do all which may achieve and cherish a just and lasting peace among ourselves and with all nations."

COULDN'T BE FOOLED

One of his friends tells of the first time he remembers seeing Lincoln. "I was a small boy," he says, "and I had gone with my father to attend some kind of an election. A neighbor, James Larkins, was present. He was a great hand to brag about anything he owned, and this time it happened to be his horse.

" 'I have the best horse in the country,' he shouted to the young Lincoln. 'I ran him nine miles in exactly three minutes, and he never fetched a long breath.'

" 'But I imagine,' Abe said dryly, 'that he fetched a good many short ones.' "

"HONEST ABE"

During the year that Lincoln spent in the store of Denton Offutt, he had made many friends and acquaintances who stood him in good stead, but he had also studied hard, mastering English grammar and reading as many books as he could get his hands on. He was appreciated and respected for his brains, his muscle and his integrity. It was while he was working in this store that he acquired the nickname "Honest Abe," and throughout his life it was always appropriate. He was called upon to arbitrate disputes, referee fights, umpire games, and judge races. With all his sterling qualities, he was modest, kind and gentle.

HE CARRIED A DRUNK ON HIS BACK

One day he helped some neighbors put up the frame of a new house—they called it a "raising"—and in the evening while he was walking home with some companions he found a stray horse, without a rider but with saddle and bridle. He recognized the horse as the property of a man who, following a well-established precedent, was probably tight.

So he looked about him and presently found the drunk, who had passed out and was lying on the ground. His companions urged him to leave the man to his fate, but Lincoln picked him up, swung him to his broad shoulders, and carried him eighty rods to the nearest house. Then he sent word to his father that he would not return until morning, and spent the night helping the drinker to get back to normal.

LINCOLN EARNS HIS FIRST DOLLAR

One evening in the White House, Lincoln said to his Secretary of State, "Seward, you never heard, did you, how I earned my first dollar?"

Seward said he hadn't, so Lincoln proceeded with the story:

"I belonged, you know, to what they called down South the 'scrubs.' We had succeeded in raising, chiefly by my labor, sufficient produce, as I thought, to justify me in taking it down the river to sell.

"After much persuasion, I got the consent of mother to go, and constructed a little flatboat, large enough to take a barrel or two of things that we had gathered, with myself and little bundle, down to the Southern market. A steamer was coming down the river. We have, you know, no wharves on the Western streams; and the custom was, if passengers were at any of the landings, for them to go out in a boat, the steamer stopping and taking them on board.

"I was contemplating my new flatboat, and wondering whether I could make it strong or improve it in any particular, when two men came down to the shore in carriages with trunks, and looking at the different boats singled out mine, and asked, 'Who owns this?' I answered, somewhat modestly, 'I do.' 'Will you,' said one of them, 'take us and our trunks out to the steamer?' 'Certainly,' said I. I was very glad to have the chance of earning something. I supposed that each of them would give me one or two or three bits. The trunks were put on my flat-boat, the passengers seated themselves on the trunks, and I sculled them out to the steamboat.

"They got on board, and I lifted up their heavy trunks, and put them on deck. The steamer was about to put on steam again, when I called out that they had forgotten to pay me. Each of them took from his pocket a silver half-dollar, and threw it on the floor of my boat. I could scarcely believe my eyes when I picked up the money. Gentlemen, you may think it was a very little thing, and in these days it seems to me a trifle; but it was a most important incident in my life. I could scarcely credit that I, a poor boy, had earned a dollar. The world seemed wider and fairer before me. I was a more hopeful and confident being from that time."

HOW HE PAID FOR A DAMAGED BOOK

Young Lincoln had borrowed a copy of Weems' Life of Washington from a neighboring farmer named Crawford. While he was reading it he left it for a time near an open window. There was a sudden rainstorm, and the book was virtually ruined. Lincoln felt very bad about it, the more so because he had no money to pay for the volume. He went to Mr. Crawford with the book and explained how the accident had happened through his own neglect. He told him of his financial condition and offered to "work out" the book's value.

Mr. Crawford thought the matter over carefully, and finally said:

"Well, Abe, as it's you, I won't be hard on you. Just

come over and pull fodder for me for two days, and we will call our accounts even."

Lincoln accepted the offer and fulfilled his obligation.

HE TOLD THIS ON HIMSELF

Once when he was riding on a stage, an old Kentuckian offered him a chew of tobacco. Lincoln politely refused, whereupon a drink of brandy was proffered. Lincoln didn't take this either. The Kentuckian showed surprise but held his tongue, but later in the afternoon, when they separated, Lincoln's friend shook hands with him warmly, spat out a mouthful of tobacco juice, and said:

"See here, stranger; you're a clever but curious companion. I may never see you again, and I don't want to offend you, but I want to say this: My experience has taught me that a man who has no vices has damned few virtues. Good day."

BOYHOOD WIT

The following inscription, written when he was fourteen years old, was found in a copybook that Lincoln used:

> 'Tis Abraham Lincoln holds the pen,
> He will be good, but God knows when.

LINCOLN COULD BE HANDY WITH HIS FISTS

One day when he was working in Offutt's store, a tough customer entered and began to make himself very obnoxious. He used offensive language, and, as the saying goes, was "spoiling for a fight." Lincoln was waiting on some women at the time and he asked the man to hold his tongue. The bully replied that he'd like to see anyone who could keep him from talking the way he pleased.

Lincoln kept cool and told him that if he would wait until the ladies had gone, he would give him a chance to have his say and also give him whatever satisfaction he wished. When the women had left, the man became more boastful and abusive. Finally he said:

"Well, if you must be whipped, I suppose I may as well whip you as any other man."

Thereupon Lincoln yanked him out of doors, threw him on the ground and pinned him down. Then he took a handful of "smartweed" that grew near by and rubbed it in his face until the braggart bellowed in pain.

During this set-to Lincoln did not lose his temper, and when he finished the job he got some water, washed his victim's face, and did what else he could to lessen his distress. Strangely enough, the beaten man turned over a new leaf and became Lincoln's loyal friend.

HE KEPT SHOP HONESTLY

It was while he was clerking at the same Offutt's store in New Salem, Illinois, that he sold a woman a small bill of goods amounting to $2.20. After the woman had gone away, he added the items again and found that he had charged six cents too much. It was the end of a tiresome day, but when he had closed the store he walked between two and three miles to return the amount of the over-charge to the customer. Then he went home satisfied.

On another similar occasion he was about to close for the night when a woman entered and asked for half a pound of tea. The sale was made, and Lincoln went home. When he reached the store the following morning, Honest Abe found a four-ounce weight on the scales. He immediately saw the mistake he had made, so he shut up the store and walked a long distance to deliver the remaining quarter-pound of tea.

LINCOLN'S INGENUITY

One of Mr. Lincoln's early friends said that the first time he ever saw the future President was when he was in the Sangamon River with his trousers rolled up and trying to pilot a flatboat over a mill dam. The boat was difficult to manage, for it was nearly full of water. By dint of hard work Lincoln got the prow of the boat over the dam, and then instead of laboriously bailing out the water, bored a hole through the forward part and let the water run out. Thus he was able to lighten the craft so that the rest of the job was comparatively easy.

HE KNEW HOW TO WRESTLE

When Lincoln lived at New Salem, Illinois, there was a group of rowdies in and around the village known as the Clary's Grove Boys. They were both tough and courageous and ruled the region with a high hand. Any man who failed to acknowledge their leadership was taken out and flogged.

Each stranger to the district was expected to have his mettle tried by this group in one way or another—by fighting, wrestling or running a race with one of them. They knew that Abraham Lincoln would be something of a problem, so they selected their champion, Jack Armstrong, to lay him on his back.

Lincoln knew what was coming, and he entered into it with alacrity. The bout began. Soon Armstrong realized that he had met his match. Lincoln had him at a distinct disadvantage, but the rest of the gang, who were looking on, struck the better man and disabled him. Then by "legging" him, Armstrong got him down.

The tables were turned, however, when Lincoln, instead of losing his temper, began to laugh and joke about the position he was in. The crowd of toughs were so impressed by the way he took it that almost immediately they invited him to become one of the gang.

LINCOLN MIGHT HAVE BEEN A BLACKSMITH

In fact, Mr. Lincoln seriously considered learning the blacksmith's trade, for he was hard up and that line of business seemed to offer the quickest money. About this time, however, a storekeeper named Reuben Radford, in New Salem, had incurred the enmity of the Clary's Grove Boys and they had been breaking his windows with considerable regularity. Radford decided to sell out his store, and a friend of Lincoln named Greene bought it for $400. Lincoln in turn offered the buyer $125 and took over the notes that had been given Radford in payment.

He took in a man named Berry as his partner, but he proved to be a wastrel, and all that Lincoln got out of the whole transaction was some good but hard-earned experience and a debt that took him years to pay.

AS A CAPTAIN IN THE BLACK HAWK WAR

When Governor Reynolds issued a call for volunteers, many of them came from New Salem and Clary's Grove, and among the first to enlist was Abraham Lincoln. When the company was full, a meeting was held for the election of officers. Lincoln was well liked, and the men told him that he must be their captain. Although he did not aspire to the rank, he consented to be a candidate. There was one other candidate, a Mr. Kirkpatrick, an influential man in the county, but Lincoln received three out of every four votes.

Kirkpatrick had once been Lincoln's employer, but the relationship had ceased when his treatment had become too overbearing to endure. Now Lincoln would have an opportunity to show that he had the upper hand. But revenge was never a part of his nature, and his former taskmaster did not have to suffer any humiliation.

LINCOLN BECAME AN INVENTOR

Lincoln not only had the aptitude with tools that the pioneer must have to live, but he had considerable mechanical genius as well. When he became involved in political and professional affairs he often found escape in working out inventions of one kind and another.

During his river days he had found plenty of grief in navigating through low water and in getting stuck on shoals and bars that shifted according to the vagaries of the river. He therefore invented an apparatus that could be folded to the boat's hull like a bellows and inflated so that it would lift the craft over such obstructions as it met.

In the Patent Office at Washington there is a model of this gadget that was whittled out by Lincoln himself. He obtained a patent on it, but the navigation of Middle Western rivers was not perceptibly influenced by the invention.

CAPTAIN LINCOLN SAVES AN INDIAN

When Lincoln was a captain in the Black Hawk War, one day an old Indian who was feeble and hungry strayed into the camp. The soldiers jumped to the conclusion that he was a spy and were on the verge of killing him when the old savage produced a letter from under the folds of his blanket. It proved to be a note from General Cass recommending him for past valuable services to the white settlers.

The men were not appeased, however, for they took the stand that the letter was a forgery and that the Indian was a spy. They were preparing to treat him as such when their tall, lanky Captain hove in sight, seething with rage. He stepped between them and the trembling Indian and ordered them to desist, which they did sullenly. The Indian proceeded on his way.

A LINCOLNIAN RETORT

Lincoln on one occasion was charged by a Major Hill with making defamatory statements about Mrs. Hill. The language used by the Major was vitriolic, and it poured forth in a steady stream. Lincoln did not lose his temper, but when he was able to get a word in edgewise he denied the allegations with emphasis. He insisted that he had a very high regard for Mrs. Hill, and he could think of absolutely nothing against her except the fact that she was Major Hill's wife.

LINCOLN AS A DUELIST

In 1839 General Shields was Auditor of the State of Illinois. He was considered a dashing young fellow, especially by the ladies. During the summer of 1842 the Springfield Journal carried a series of letters by someone writing under the pen name of "Aunt Becca." In one of them the dashing young Auditor was described as "a ballroom dandy, floatin' about on the earth without heft or substance, just like a lot of cat fur where cats had been fightin'."

As might be expected, these letters caused a great furor in Springfield. No one knew who their author was, but Shields let it be known that if he found out who wrote them, he would challenge the writer to a duel. "Aunt Becca" didn't help matters any when she wrote another letter making a humble apology and offering to let Shields squeeze her hand by way of satisfaction. She proceeded:

"If this should not answer, there is one thing more I would rather do than get a lickin'. I have all along expected to die a widow; but, as Mr. Shields is rather good-looking than otherwise, I must say I don't care if we compromise the matter by—really, Mr. Printer, I can't help blushing—but I must come out—I—but widowed modesty—well, if I must, I must—wouldn't he—maybe sorter let the old grudge drap if I was to consent to be—be—his wife? I know he is a fightin' man, and would rather fight than eat; but isn't marryin' better than fightin', though it does sometimes run into it? And I don't think, upon the whole, I'd be sich a bad match neither; I'm not over sixty, and am just four feet three in my bare feet, and not much more around the girth; and for color, I wouldn't turn my back to nary a girl in the Lost Townships. But, after all, maybe I'm counting my chickens before they're hatched, and dreamin' of matrimonial bliss when the only alternative reserved for me may be a lickin'. Jeff tells me the way these fire-eaters do is to give the challenged party the choice of weapons, which being the case, I tell you in confidence, I never fight with anything but broomsticks or hot water, or a shovelful of coals, or some such thing; the former of which, being somewhat like a shillelah, may not be so very objectionable to him. I will give him a choice, however, in one thing, and that is whether, when we fight, I shall wear breeches or he petticoats, for I presume this change is sufficient to place us on an equality."

It developed that the real author of these letters was Miss Mary Todd, to whom Abraham Lincoln was then engaged to be married. For this reason he felt that he was in honor bound to assume the responsibility of her acid pen. Lincoln accepted the challenge, and the two men actually were on their way to shoot it out when better sense prevailed and the affair was ended without recourse to pistols and coffee for two.

HE HAD A SELFISH STREAK

Dressed in a new suit of clothes that he had acquired at some pains and not a little expense, Lincoln was riding horseback past a deep slough in which there was a seriously mired pig. His first impulse was to stop and extricate the animal from a really critical situation, but he decided against it because of his new clothes.

But as the young lawyer jogged along the road he could not rid his mind of the vision of the hapless animal dying a slow death in the mudhole. After riding fully two miles further, he turned back and, with considerable difficulty and the virtual ruination of his suit, released the pig from its predicament.

As he rode away from the scene he began to ponder his motive in returning to save the pig. At first he attributed it to sheer benevolence, but Lincoln was not a self back-patter, and this explanation did not satisfy him. Presently he came to the conclusion that going to the pig's relief was pure selfishness, for, as he explained to a friend, "It was to take a pain out of my own mind."

HE LOVED HIS STEPMOTHER

The tradition that stepmothers are cold and heartless toward their husbands' children by former marriages did not hold in the Lincoln family. The future President of the United States loved the woman his father married, and his regard for her could scarcely have been warmer if she had been his actual mother.

Shortly after Mr. Lincoln began practicing law at Springfield, Illinois, he won a criminal case for which he received a fee of $500. The following morning one of his lawyer friends called on him at his office and found him sitting at a table counting his money.

"Look at this, Judge," he said with awe in his voice. "See what a heap of money I've got from the Blank case. Did you ever see anything like it? Why, I never had so much money in my life before, put it all together." Then he said soberly:

"I have got just $500; if it were only $750, I would go directly and purchase a quarter-section of land, and settle it on my old stepmother."

His friend said that he would loan him the difference and take his note for it, to which Lincoln immediately agreed. Then the other lawyer, thinking to give him some good advice, said:

"Lincoln, I would not do just what you have indicated. Your stepmother is getting old, and probably will not live many years. I would settle the property upon her for her use during her lifetime, to revert to you upon her death."

Lincoln bridled at this:

"I shall do no such thing," he said. "It is a poor return at best for all the good woman's devotion and fidelity to me, and there is not going to be any halfway business about it."

And there wasn't!

THERE WAS SOMETHING ELSE AGAIN

One day Lincoln assisted in the prosecution of a man accused of raiding a neighbor's hen-roost. Later he told his friends, with much amusement, of how he jogged along homeward with the foreman of the jury who had convicted the thief. Lincoln complimented the foreman on the verdict, whereat his companion observed:

"Why, when the country was young, and I was stronger than I am now, I didn't mind packing off a sheep now and then, but as for stealing hens—"

The man spat in contempt of anyone who could sink so low as that!

LINCOLN UNDERSTOOD ORDINARY PEOPLE

On at least one occasion Lincoln gave some good advice to a young lawyer.

"Billy," he said, "don't shoot too high—aim lower, and the common people will understand you.

"They are the ones you want to reach—at least, they are the ones you ought to reach.

"The educated and refined people will understand you anyway. If you aim too high, your idea will go over the heads of the masses and hit only those who need no hitting."

LINCOLN KNEW HUMAN NATURE.

Lincoln's legal opponent in a certain case undoubtedly had the law on his side. He knew it, and Lincoln knew it.

The day was warm and sultry. The courtroom was stifling, and perspiration rolled down the brows of everyone there. As the opponent proceeded with his vociferous arguments, he became so uncomfortable that he removed his coat and vest. This was not unusual in that day at that time of year. But in so doing, he displayed a shirt that was buttoned in the back.

This style of haberdashery was wholly out of keeping with the trend of the times, and Lincoln, realizing primitive people's prejudice against such sartorial innovations, made capital out of it. When he had the floor he said:

"Gentlemen of the jury, having justice on my side, I

don't think you will be at all influenced by the gentleman's pretended knowledge of the law when you see he does not even know which side of his shirt should be in front."

There was an uproarious laugh from all corners of the courtroom, including the jury box, and Lincoln won the case.

LINCOLN AND MONEY MATTERS

As a usual thing, Lincoln left all financial matters pertaining to his law business to his partner. It is said that he never entered any item in the account book. When someone would make a payment to him for legal help, he would at once divide it with his partner. And if his partner was absent, Lincoln would wrap his share in a piece of paper, mark it "Case of Jones vs. Brown—Herndon's half," and deposit it in his drawer.

JUSTICE IN A MURDER CASE

In the early days Lincoln had had trouble with the "Clary Grove Boys." Because he had kept his temper he had not only come out on top, but he had made some excellent friends as well. One of them, Jack Armstrong, grew up and had a son, the oldest of whom became involved in a fight that resulted in the death of a young man of the neighborhood. Young Armstrong was charged with striking the blow that caused his death.

Lincoln wrote a letter to his mother volunteering to defend her son. It looked like a hopeless task. A fair trial seemed like too much to expect on account of the ferment in the region. Lincoln obtained a postponement of the trial and also a change in the place where it was to be held.

When the case came to trial the chief witness testified that "by the aid of the brightly shining moon" he saw the prisoner inflict the death blow with a slung shot.

It looked bad for the prisoner, but Lincoln was equal to the occasion. He proved conclusively by the almanac that there could not possibly have been a moon shining at that time of month, and after half an hour the jury brought in a verdict of "Not guilty."

MRS. LINCOLN PUT ONE OVER ON ABE

Late one night Lincoln returned home after a long trip on business to a neighboring county. He got off his horse at the familiar corner and turned to enter his house, but he stopped short. He had never seen the house before in his life. Other houses in the neighborhood seemed familiar, so he stopped in at one of them. He knocked at the door.

"Who's there?"

"Abe Lincoln," he answered. "I am looking for my house. I thought it was across the way, but when I went away a few weeks ago, there was only a one-story house there, and now there are two stories. I think I must be lost."

The neighbors explained that Mrs. Lincoln had added a story in his absence.

WHEN LINCOLN TRADED HORSES

In a bantering session on the subject of horse trading,

Lincoln made an agreement with a certain judge in Illinois to make a trade with him under the following conditions: each was to bring a horse the following morning at nine o'clock. There were no stipulations as to the kind or condition, and neither man was to see the other's horse until the time specified. If either backed out, he was to pay a forfeit of $25.

At the appointed hour the Judge appeared leading a nag that was so skinny that one could count all his ribs; an ancient plug that wobbled and creaked in every joint. After a few minutes Lincoln arrived. He was carrying a wooden sawhorse on his shoulders.

A tremendous laugh went up. Lincoln's face fell when he saw the Judge's horse.

"Judge," he said, "I'll give you my word, this is the first time I ever got the worst of it in a horse trade."

HUMOR FROM A DEBATE WITH DOUGLAS

"Fellow-citizens: My friend, Mr. Douglas, made the startling announcement today that the Whigs are all dead.

"If that be so, fellow-citizens, you will now experience the novelty of hearing a speech from a dead man; and I suppose you might properly say, in the language of the old hymn:

" 'Hark! from the tombs a doleful sound.' "

LINCOLN CITES A PARALLEL

Replying to a statement by Douglas regarding trust in Providence during the campaign of 1852, Lincoln made this reply:

"Let us stand by our candidate [General Scott] as faithfully as he has always stood by our country, and I much doubt if we do not perceive a slight abatement of Judge Douglas's confidence in Providence as well as the people.

"I suspect that confidence is not more firmly fixed with the Judge than it was with the old woman whose horse ran away with her in a buggy. She said she 'trusted in Providence till the britchen broke,' and then 'she didn't know what on airth to do.'

"The chance is, the Judge will see the britchen broke, and then he can, at his leisure, bewail the fate of Locofocoism as the victim of misplaced confidence."

NEGRO VERSUS CROCODILE

Lincoln was always quick to point out the fallacy of a statement with which he did not agree. In one of his speeches Douglas said:

"As between the crocodile and the Negro, I take the side of the Negro; but as between the Negro and the white man—I would go for the white man every time."

"I believe," said Lincoln, "that this is a sort of proposition in proportion, which may be stated thus:

"As the Negro is to the white man, so is the crocodile to the Negro; and as the Negro may rightfully treat the crocodile as a beast or reptile, so the white man may rightfully treat the Negro as a beast or reptile."

Thus, reasoning from Douglas's own hypothesis, Lincoln proved that his opponent's statement was a shallow one.

HOW LINCOLN IMPRESSED A NEW YORKER

The following description of Lincoln was written by a man who listened to one of his speeches in New York City:

"When Lincoln rose to speak, I was greatly disappointed. He was tall, tall, oh, so tall, and so angular and awkward that I had for an instant a feeling of pity for so ungainly a man. He began in a low tone of voice, as if he were used to speaking out of doors, and was afraid of speaking too loud.

"He said 'Mr. Cheerman,' instead of 'Mr. Chairman,' and employed many other words with an old-fashioned pronunciation. I said to myself, 'Old fellow, you won't do; it is all very well for the Wild West, but this will never go down in New York.' But pretty soon he began to get into the subject; he straightened up, made regular and graceful gestures; his face lighted as with an inward fire; the whole man was transfigured. I forgot the clothing, his personal appearance, and his individual peculiarities. Presently, forgetting myself, I was on my feet with the rest, yelling like a wild Indian, cheering the wonderful man. In the close parts of his argument, you could hear the gentle sizzling of the gas burners.

"When he reached a climax, the thunders of applause were terrific. It was a great speech. When I came out of the hall my face was glowing with excitement and my frame all aquiver. A friend, with his eyes aglow, asked me what I thought of Abe Lincoln, the rail-splitter. I said, 'He's the greatest man since St. Paul.' And I think so yet."

MR. LINCOLN HAS A VISION

Lincoln was tired when he returned home after hearing of his nomination for the Presidency. He went to his wife's sitting room and lay down. The couch on which he reclined was directly opposite the looking-glass of a bureau. Let him tell the story:

"As I reclined, my eye fell upon the glass, and I saw distinctly two images of myself, exactly alike, except that one was a little paler than the other. I arose and lay down again with the same result. It made me quite uncomfortable for a few minutes, but, some friends coming in, the matter passed out of my mind. The next day, while walking in the street, I was suddenly reminded of the circumstance, and the disagreeable sensation produced by it returned. I had never seen anything of the kind before, and did not know what to make of it. I determined to go home and place myself in the same position, and, if the same effect was produced, I would make up my mind that it was the natural result of some principle of refraction or optics, which I did not understand, and dismiss it. I tried the experiment, with the same result; and, as I had said to myself, accounted for it on some principle unknown to me, and it then ceased to trouble me. But the God who works through the laws of Nature might surely give a sign to me, if one of His chosen servants, even through the operation of a principle in optics."

Lincoln said to his friend Noah Brookes: "I should be the most presumptuous blockhead upon this footstool if I for one day thought that I could discharge the duties which have come upon me, since I came to this place, without the aid and enlightenment of One who is stronger and wiser than all others." He said on another occasion: "I am very sure that if I do not go away from here a wiser man, I shall go away a better man, from having learned here what a very poor sort of a man I am."

TWO EVIDENCES OF LINCOLN'S GOOD NATURE

Springfield, Illinois, was very proud of Abraham Lincoln when he was nominated for President, and the authorities set aside the Executive Chamber in the State House for his use in receiving callers. An eye-witness relates two incidents that reveal his character.

"Mr. Lincoln being in conversation with a gentleman one day, two raw, plainly dressed young men entered the room, and bashfully lingered near the door. As soon as he observed them, and apprehended their embarrassment, he rose and walked to them, saying: 'How do you do, my good fellows? What can I do for you? Will you sit down?' The spokesman of the pair, the shorter of the two, declined to sit, and explained the object of the call thus: He had had a talk about the relative height of Mr. Lincoln and his companion, and had asserted his belief that they were of exactly the same height. He had come in to verify his judgment, Mr. Lincoln smiled, went and got his cane, and, placing the end of it upon the wall, said:

" 'Here, young man, come under here.'

"The young man came under the cane as Mr. Lincoln held it, and when it was perfectly adjusted to his height, Mr. Lincoln said:

" 'Now come out, and hold the cane.'

"This he did, while Mr. Lincoln stood under. Rubbing

his head back and forth to see that it worked easily under the measurement, he stepped out, and declared to the sagacious fellow who was curiously looking on that he had guessed with remarkable accuracy—that he and the young man were exactly the same height. Then he shook hands with them and sent them on their way. Mr. Lincoln would just as soon have thought of cutting off his right hand as he would have thought of turning those boys away with the impression that they had in any way insulted his dignity.

"They had hardly disappeared when an old and modestly dressed woman made her appearance. She knew Mr. Lincoln, but Mr. Lincoln did not at first recognize her. Then she undertook to recall to his memory certain incidents connected with his ride upon the circuit—especially his dining at her house upon the road at different times. Then he remembered her and her home. Having fixed her own place in his recollection, she tried to recall to him a certain scanty dinner of bread and milk that he once ate at her house. He could not remember it—on the contrary, he only remembered that he had always fared well at her house.

" 'Well,' said she, 'one day you came along after we had got through dinner, and we had eaten up everything, and I could give you nothing but a bowl of bread and milk, and you ate it; when you got up you said it was good enough for the President of the United States!'

"The good woman had come in from the country, making a journey of eight or ten miles, to relate to Mr. Lincoln this incident, which, in her mind, had doubtless taken the form of a prophecy. Mr. Lincoln placed the honest creature at her ease, chatted with her of old times, and dismissed her in the most happy and complacent frame of mind."

AND HE REALLY BELIEVED IT

In early 1860 the name of Abraham Lincoln was being mentioned in connection with the Presidential nomination. The lanky Illinois lawyer was, quite naturally, proud of even this distinction, for it placed him in the category of some very great men. But, in public at least, he wore the cloak of humility, and when someone spoke to him about the possibility of his carrying the banner, his answer was discouraging. On one such occasion he replied:

"In regard to the matter you spoke of, I beg you will not give it further mention. Seriously, I do not think I am fit for the Presidency."

IN NEW YORK'S SLUMS

The section known as Five Points, in 1860, was perhaps New York's most criminal neighborhood. One Sunday Lincoln went alone to visit its House of Industry. Let the Superintendent of the Sabbath School tell of his visit:

"One Sunday morning I saw a tall, remarkable-looking man enter the room and take a seat among us. He listened with fixed attention to our exercises, and his countenance expressed such genuine interest that I approached him and suggested that he might be willing to say something to the children. He accepted the invitation with evident pleasure, and coming forward began a simple address, which at once fascinated every little hearer and hushed the room into silence. His language was strikingly beautiful, and his tones musical with intense feeling. The little faces would droop into sad conviction when he uttered sentences of warning, and would brighten into sunshine as he spoke cheerful words of promise. Once or twice he attempted to close his remarks, but the imperative shout of, 'Go on! Oh, do go on!' would compel him to resume.

"As I looked upon the gaunt and sinewy frame of the stranger, and marked his powerful head and determined features, now touched into softness by the impressions of the moment, I felt an irrepressible curiosity to learn something more about him, and while he was quietly leaving the room, I begged a man to tell me his name. He replied: 'It is Abraham Lincoln, from Illinois.' "

LINCOLN TOLD THIS ON HIMSELF

Said he: "In the days when I used to be on the circuit, I was accosted in the cars by a stranger, who said, 'Excuse me, sir, but I have an article in my possession which belongs to you.' 'How is that?' I asked, considerably astonished.

"The stranger took a jackknife from his pocket. 'This knife,' said he, 'was placed in my hands some years ago, with the injunction that I was to keep it until I had found a man uglier than myself. I have carried it from that time to this. Allow me to say, sir, that I think you are fairly entitled to the property.' "

A SOUTHERNER'S ESTIMATE OF LINCOLN

The following story was told by a resident of Springfield, Illinois, three-quarters of a century ago:

"An old man hailing from Mississippi, dressed in plain homespun, came to our city Saturday. He mingled freely with the Republican Representatives, got their news, and seemed to think we are not quite so black as we are represented.

"He called on Mr. Lincoln, talked freely with him, and heard the President-elect express his sentiments and intentions. He learned that Mr. Lincoln entertained none but the kindest feelings towards the people of the South, and that he would protect the South in her just rights.

"He had a long conversation, and went away delighted. He left the office of Mr. Lincoln in company with a friend, who communicated this to us, and when outside the door he remarked, while the tears stole down his furrowed cheeks: 'Oh! if the people of the South could hear what I have heard, they would love and not hate Mr. Lincoln. I will tell my friends at home; but,' he added sorrowfully, 'they will not believe me.' He said that he did wish that every man in the South could be personally acquainted with Mr. Lincoln."

GREAT SENTIMENTS UTTERED BY THE RAILSPLITTER

"The Union must be, should be, preserved.

"We are not enemies, but friends. We must not be enemies. Though passion may have strained, it must not break our bonds of affection.

"The mystic chords of memory, stretching from every

battlefield and patriotic grave to every living heart and hearthstone all over this broad land, will yet swell the chorus of the Union, when again touched, as surely they will be.

"As the country has placed me at the helm of the ship, I'll try to steer her through.

"Die when I may, I want it said of me by those who know me best that I have always plucked a thistle and planted a flower when I thought a flower would grow.

"In this extraordinary war," said he, "extraordinary developments have manifested themselves, such as have not been seen in former wars; and among these manifestations nothing has been more remarkable than these fairs for the relief of suffering soldiers and their families. And the chief agent in these fairs are the women of America. I am not accustomed to the use of language of eulogy; I have never studied the art of paying compliments to women; but I must say that if all that has been said by orators and poets since the creation of the world, in praise of women, were applied to the women of America, it would not do them justice for their conduct during the war. I will close by saying, God bless the women of America!"

GENERAL GRANT'S WHISKEY

A short time before the fall of Vicksburg, a group of sincere and pious teetotalers visited Lincoln and urged the removal of General Grant on the ground that he drank too much whiskey.

Lincoln appeared to be very much interested. His face lit up as he replied:

"Ah, gentlemen, can you tell me where General Grant obtains his whiskey?

They couldn't, of course, so Lincoln continued:

"Because if I can find out, I am going to send every general in the field a barrel of it!"

LINCOLN HONORED BY THE NEGROES OF RICHMOND

The following moving incident is related by a contemporary named G. F. Shepley:

"After Mr. Lincoln's interview with Judge Campbell, the President being about to return to the Wabash, I took him and Admiral Porter in my carriage. An immense concourse of colored people thronged the streets, accompanied and followed the carriage, calling upon the President with the wildest exclamations of gratitude and delight.

"He was the Moses, the Messiah, to the slaves of the South. Hundreds of colored women tossed their hands high in the air and bent down to the ground, weeping for joy. Some shouted songs of deliverance, and sang the old plantation refrains, which prophesied the coming of a deliverer from bondage. 'God bless you, Father Abraham!' went up from a thousand throats.

"Those only who have seen the paroxysmal enthusiasm of a religious meeting of slaves can form an adequate conception of the way in which tears and smiles, and shouts of the emancipated people evinced the frenzy of their gratitude to their deliverer. He looked at all attentively, with a face expressive only of a sort of pathetic wonder.

"Occasionally its sadness would alternate with one

of his peculiar smiles, and he would remark on the great proportion of those whose color indicated a mixed lineage from the white master and the black slave; and that reminded him of some little story of his life in Kentucky, which he would smilingly tell; and then his face would relapse again into that sad expression which all will remember who saw him during the last few weeks of the Rebellion. Perhaps it was a presentiment of his impending fate.

"I accompanied him to the ship, bade him farewell and left him, to see his face no more. Not long after, the bullet of the assassin arrested the beatings of one of the kindest hearts that ever throbbed in human bosom.

LINCOLN'S LETTERS

LETTER TO MRS. ARMSTRONG

Springfield, Ill., Sept. —, 18—.

Dear Mrs. Armstrong: I have just heard of your deep affliction, and the arrest of your son for murder.

I can hardly believe that he can be guilty of the crime alleged against him.

It does not seem possible. I am anxious that he should have a fair trial, at any rate; and gratitude for your long-continued kindness to me in adverse circumstances prompts me to offer my humble services gratuitously in his behalf.

It will afford me an opportunity to requite, in a small degree, the favors I received at your hand, and that of your lamented husband, when your roof afforded me grateful shelter, without money and without price.

Yours truly,
A. LINCOLN.

AFFECTIONATE SON

Lincoln wrote the following at the close of a letter to his stepbrother, John Johnston, regarding his father, Mr. Lincoln, the poor ne'er-do-well, who was ill:

"I sincerely hope father may yet recover his health; but at all events, tell him to remember to call upon, and confide in, our great and good merciful Maker, who will not turn away from him in any extremity.

"He notes the fall of the sparrow, and numbers the hairs of our heads, and He will not forget the dying man who puts his trust in Him.

"Say to him that, if we could meet now, it is doubtful whether it would not be more painful than pleasant, but that if it is his lot to go now, he will soon have a joyful meeting with loved ones gone before, and where the rest of us, through the mercy of God, hope ere long to join them."

LINCOLN WRITES HIS STEPMOTHER

Lincoln's love for his second mother was most filial and affectionate. In a letter of November 4, 1851, just after the death of his father, he writes to her as follows:

"Dear Mother: Chapman tells me that he wants you to go and live with him. If I were you, I would try it a while. If you get tired of it (as I think you will not), you can return to your own home. Chapman feels very kindly to you, and I have no doubt he will make your situation very pleasant.

"Sincerely your son,
"A. Lincoln."

LINCOLN'S IDEA OF THE SLAVERY CONFLICT IN 1855

Springfield, Ill., August 15, 1855.

Hon. George Robertson, Lexington, Ky.

My Dear Sir: The volume you left for me has been received. I am really grateful for the honor of your kind remembrance, as well as for the book.

The partial reading I have already given it has afforded me much of both pleasure and instruction. It was new to me that the exact question which led to the Missouri Compromise had arisen before it arose in regard to Missouri, and that you had taken so prominent a part in it. Your short but able and patriotic speech on that occasion has not been improved upon since by those holding the same views; and with all the light you then had, the views you took appear to me as very reasonable.

You are not a friend of slavery in the abstract. In that speech you spoke of the "peaceful extinction of slavery," and used other expressions indicating your belief that the thing was, at some time, to have an end. Since then we have had thirty-six years of experience; and this experience has demonstrated, I think, that there is no peaceful extinction of slavery in prospect for us.

The signal failure of Henry Clay and other good and great men, in 1849, to effect anything in favor of a gradual emancipation in Kentucky, together with a thousand other signs, extinguished that hope utterly. On the question of liberty, as a principle, we are not what we have been.

When we were the political slaves of King George, and wanted to be free, we called the maxim that "all men are created equal" a self-evident truth, but now, when we have grown fat, and have lost all dread of being slaves ourselves, we have become so greedy to be *masters* that we call the same maxim a "self-evident lie."

The Fourth of July has not quite dwindled away, it is still a great day for burning firecrackers!

That spirit which desired the peaceful extinction of slavery has itself become extinct with the occasion and the men of the Revolution. Under the impulse of that occasion, nearly half the States adopted systems of emancipation at once; and it is a significant fact that not a single State has done the like since.

So far as peaceful, voluntary emancipation is concerned, the condition of the Negro slave in America, scarcely less terrible to the contemplation of a free mind, is now as fixed and hopeless of change for the better as that of the lost souls of the finally impenitent. The Autocrat of all the Russians will resign his crown and proclaim his subjects free republicans sooner than will our American masters voluntarily give up their slaves.

Our political problem now is, "Can we, as a nation, continue together permanently—forever—half slave and half free?"

The problem is too mighty for me. May God, in His mercy, superintend the solution.

Your much obliged friend, and humble servant,

A. LINCOLN.

Springfield, Ill., April 6, 1859.

Gentlemen: Your kind note inviting me to attend a festival in Boston on the 13th instant, in honor of the birthday of Thomas Jefferson, was duly received. My engagements are such that I cannot attend.

The Democracy of to-day hold the liberty of one man to be absolutely nothing, when in conflict with another man's right of property. Republicans, on the contrary, are both for the man and the dollar, but, in case of conflict, the man before the dollar.

I remember once being much amused at seeing two partially intoxicated men engaged in a fight with their great-coats on, which fight, after a long and rather harmless contest, ended in each having fought himself out of his own coat, and into that of the other. If the two leading parties of this day are really identical with the two in the days of Jefferson and Adams, they have performed the same feat as the two drunken men.

But, soberly, it is now no child's play to save the principles of Jefferson from total overthrow in this nation. . . . This is a world of compensations; and he who would be no slave must consent to have no slave. Those who deny freedom to others deserve it not for themselves; and, under a just God, cannot long retain it.

All honor to Jefferson; to a man who, in the concrete pressure of a struggle for national independence by a single people, had the coolness, foresight, and capacity to introduce into a merely revolutionary document an abstract truth, applicable to all men and all times, and so to embalm it there that to-day and in all coming days it shall be a rebuke and stumbling-block to the harbingers of reappearing tyranny and oppression.

Your obedient servant,

A. LINCOLN.

Messrs. H. L. Pierce, and others, etc.

LINCOLN'S FIRST LETTER OF ACCEPTANCE

Springfield, Ill., May 25, 1860.

Hon. George Ashman, President of the Republican National Convention.

Sir: I accept the nomination tendered me by the Convention over which you preside, and of which I am formally apprised in the letter of yourself and others, acting as a committee of the Convention for that purpose.

The declaration of principles and sentiments, which

accompanies your letter, meets my approval; and it shall be my care not to violate or disregard it in any part. Imploring the assistance of Divine Providence, and with due regard to the views and feelings of all who were represented in the Convention; to the rights of all the States and Territories and people of the nation; to the inviolability of the Constitution; and the perpetual union, harmony and prosperity of all, I am now happy to cooperate for the practical success of the principles declared by the Convention.

Your obliged friend, and fellow citizen,

A. Lincoln.

MR. LINCOLN'S REPLY TO THE POET, BRYANT

Springfield, Ill., June 28, 1860.

Please accept my thanks for the honor done me by your kind letter of the 16th. I appreciate the danger against which you would guard me; nor am I wanting in the purpose to avoid it. I thank you for the additional strength your words give me to maintain that purpose.

Your friend and servant.

A. Lincoln.

LETTER TO GENERAL DUFF GREEN

Springfield, Ill., Dec. 28, 1860.

Gen. Duff Green.

My Dear Sir: I do not desire any amendment of the Constitution. Recognizing, however, that questions of such amendment rightfully belong to the American people, I should not feel justified nor inclined to withhold from them, if I could, a fair opportunity of expressing their will thereon through either of the modes prescribed in the instrument.

In addition, I declare that the maintenance inviolate of the rights of the States, and especially the right of each State, to order and control its own domestic institutions, according to its own judgment exclusively, is essential to the balance of powers on which the perfection and endurance of our political fabric depend; and I denounce the lawless invasion by armed force of the soil of any State or Territory, no matter under what pretext, as the gravest of crimes.

I am greatly averse to writing anything for the public at this time; and I consent to the publication of this only upon the condition that six of the twelve United States Senators for the States of Georgia, Alabama, Mississippi, Louisiana, Florida, and Texas shall sign their names to what is written on this sheet, below my name, and allow the whole to be published together.

Yours truly,
A. LINCOLN.

MR. LINCOLN'S FIRST PUBLIC LETTER AFTER HIS ELECTION

Springfield, Ill., Jan. 28, 1861.

Messrs. R. A. Cameron, Walter Marsh, and D. C. Branham, Committee.

Gentlemen: I have the honor to acknowledge the receipt by your hands of a copy of a joint resolution adopted by the Legislature of the State of Indiana, on the 15th instant, inviting me to visit that honorable body on my way to the Federal Capital.

Expressing my profound gratitude for the flattering testimonial of their regard and esteem, be pleased to bear to them my acceptance of their kind invitation, and inform them, I will comply in accordance with their expressed desire, on the 12th day of February next. With feelings of high consideration, I remain your obedient servant,

A. LINCOLN.

LINCOLN TO COLFAX

Executive Mansion, March 8, 1861.

Hon. Schuyler Colfax.

My Dear Sir: Your letter of the 6th has just been handed me by Mr. Baker, of Minnesota. When I said to you the other day that I wished to write you a letter, I had reference, of course, to my not having offered you a Cabinet appointment.

I meant to say, and now do say, you are most honorably and amply recommended; and a tender of the appointment was not withheld, in any part, because of anything happening in 1858. Indeed, I should have decided as I did easier than I did had that matter never existed. I had partly made up my mind in favor of Mr. Smith—not conclusively, of course—before your name was mentioned in that connection. When you were brought forward, I said, "Colfax is a young man, is already in position, is running a brilliant career, and is sure of a bright future in any event—with Smith it is now or never."

I considered either abundantly competent, and decided on the ground I stated.

I now have to beg that you will not do me the injustice

to suppose for a moment that I remember anything against you in malice.

Yours very truly,
A. LINCOLN.

LINCOLN TO SEWARD

The Secretary of State considered it his duty to urge the President to more energetic action, April, '61, and presented his ideas under the following head, "Some Thoughts for the President's Consideration, April 1, 1861":

"First, we are at the end of a month's administration, and yet without a policy, either domestic, foreign," etc., etc.

The President sent his reply the same day. Only the "hand of iron in the glove of velvet" could have written the answer. It was irresistible logic, faultless in tact, kind but positively firm.

The President concludes: "I remark [regarding an energetic policy] that if this must be done, I must do it. When a general line of policy is adopted I apprehend there is no danger of its being changed without good reason or continuing to be a subject of unnecessary debate. Still, on points arising in its progress, I wish, and suppose I am entitled to have, the advice of all the Cabinet.

"Your ob't serv't,
"A. LINCOLN."

Washington, Feb. 3, 1862.

General McClellan.

My Dear Sir: You and I have distinct and different plans for a movement of the Army of the Potomac—

yours to be down the Chesapeake, up the Rappahannock to Urbana and across land to the terminus of the railroad on the York River; mine to move directly to the point on the railroads southwest of Manassas.

If you will give me satisfactory answers to the following questions, I shall gladly yield my plan to yours:

First: Does not your plan involve a greatly larger expenditure of time and money than mine?

Second: Wherein is a victory more certain by your plan than mine?

Third: Wherein is a victory more valuable by your plan than mine?

Fourth: In fact, would it not be less valuable in this, that it would break no greater line of the enemies' communication, than mine would?

Fifth: In case of disaster, would not a retreat be more difficult by your plan than by mine?

Yours truly,
A. LINCOLN.

LETTER TO AUGUST BELMONT

July 31, 1862.

August Belmont, Esq.

Dear Sir: You send to Mr. W—— an extract from a letter written at New Orleans the 9th instant, which is shown to me.

You do not give the writer's name; but plainly he is a man of ability and probably of some note. He says, "The time has arrived when Mr. Lincoln must take a decisive course.

"Trying to please everybody, he will satisfy nobody.

"A vacillating policy in matters of importance is the very worst. Now is the time, if ever, for honest men who love their country to rally to its support.

"Why will not the North say officially that it wishes for the restoration of the Union as it was?"

And so it seems, this is the point in which the writer thinks I have no policy. Why will he not read and understand what I have said? The substance of the very subject he desires is in the two inaugurals, in each of the two regular messages sent to Congress, and in many, if not all, of the minor documents issued by the Executive since the inauguration.

Broken eggs cannot be mended; but Louisiana has nothing to do now but to take her place in the Union as it was, barring the already broken eggs. The sooner she does so, the smaller will be the amount of that which is past mending.

This Government cannot much longer play a game in which it stakes all, and its enemies stake nothing.

Those enemies must understand that they cannot experiment for ten years trying to destroy the Government, and, if they fail, still come back into the Union unhurt.

If they expect, in any contingency, to ever have the Union as it was, I join with the writer in saying, "Now is the time."

How much better it would have been for the writer to have gone at this under the protection of the Army at New Orleans, than to have sat in a closet writing complaining letters northward! Yours truly,

A. LINCOLN.

THE PRESIDENT ON THE NEGRO QUESTION

Executive Mansion, Washington, August 22, 1862.

Hon. Horace Greeley: I have just read yours of the 19th addressed to myself through the New York Tribune.

If there be in it any statements or assumptions of fact which I may know to be erroneous, I do not now and here controvert it.

If there be in it any inference which I believe to be falsely drawn, I do not now and here argue against it.

If there be perceptible in it an impatient and dictatorial tone, I waive it, in deference to an old friend, whose heart I have always supposed to be right.

As to the policy I "seem to be pursuing," as you say, I have not meant to leave any one in doubt. I would save the Union. I would save it in the shortest way under the Constitution. The sooner the national authority can be restored, the nearer the Union will be "the Union as it was."

If there be those who would not save the Union unless they could at the same time save slavery, I do not agree with them. If there be those who would not save the Union unless they could at the same time destroy slavery, I do not agree with them.

My paramount object in this struggle is to save the Union, and is not either to save or destroy slavery.

If I could save the Union without freeing any slave I would do it, and if I could save it by freeing all the slaves, I would do it. And if I could save it by freeing some and leaving others alone, I would also do that.

What I do about slavery and the colored race I do because I believe it helps to save the Union. And what I forbear, I forbear because I do not believe it would help to save the Union. I shall do less whenever I shall believe what I am doing hurts the cause; and I shall do more whenever I shall believe doing more will help the cause.

I shall try to correct errors when shown to be errors, and I shall adopt new views as fast as they shall appear to be true views.

I have here stated my purpose according to my views of official duty, and I intend no modification of my oft-expressed personal wish that all men everywhere should be free.

Yours,

A. LINCOLN.

PARTIAL REPLY TO CENSURE ON THE ARREST OF VALLANDIGHAM, JUNE, 1863

"Mr. Vallandigham avows his hostility to the war on the part of the Union; and his arrest was made because he was laboring, with some effect, to prevent the raising of troops, to encourage desertions from the army, and to leave the rebellion without an adequate military force to suppress it.

"He was not arrested because he was damaging the political prospects of the administration, or the personal interests of the Commanding General, but because he was damaging the army, upon the existence and vigor of which the life of the nation depends.

"He was warring upon the military, and this gave the military the Constitutional jurisdiction to lay hands upon him.

A. LINCOLN."

LETTER TO MAJOR-GENERAL HOOKER

Executive Mansion,
Washington, D. C., Jan. 26, 1863.

Major-General Hooker.

General: I have placed you at the head of the Army of the Potomac. Of course, I have done this upon what appears to me to be sufficient reasons, and yet I think it best for you to know that there are some things in regard to which I am not quite satisfied with you.

I believe you to be a brave and skillful soldier, which, of course, I like. I also believe you do not mix politics with your profession, in which you are right. You have confidence in yourself, which is a valuable, if not indispensable, quality. You are ambitious, which, within reasonable bounds, does good rather than harm. But I think that, during General Burnside's command of the Army, you have taken counsel of your ambitions, and thwarted him as much as you could, in which you did a great wrong, both to the country, and a most meritorious and honorable brother officer.

I have heard, in such a way as to believe it, of your recently saying that both the army and the Government needed a dictator. Of course, it was not for this, but in spite of it, that I have given you a command.

Only those generals who gain success can set up as dictators. What I ask of you is military success, and I will risk the dictatorship. The Government will support you to the utmost of its ability, which is neither more nor less than it has done and will do for all commanders. I much fear that the spirit that you have aided to infuse into the army, of criticising their commander, and withholding confidence from him, will now turn upon you. I shall assist you as far as I can to put it down. Neither you nor Napoleon, if he were alive again, could get any good out of an army while such a spirit prevails in it.

And now, beware of rashness! Beware of rashness! But, with energy and sleepless vigilance, go forward and give us victories.

Yours very truly,

A. LINCOLN.

THE PRESIDENT'S LETTER TO HON. JAMES C. CONKLIN, AUGUST 16, 1863

"I do not believe that any compromise embracing the maintenance of the Union is now possible.

"The strength of the rebellion is in the army. That army dominates all the country and all the people within its range. Any offer of terms made by any man or men within that range, in opposition to that army, is simply nothing for the present, because such man or men have no power whatever to enforce their side of a compromise, if one were made with them. No word or intimation from the rebel army, or from any of the men controlling it, in relation to any peace compromise, has ever come to my knowledge or belief.

"You dislike the Emancipation Proclamation, and perhaps would have it retracted. You say it is unconstitutional. I think differently. I think the Constitution invests the Commander-in-Chief with the law of war in time of war. The most that can be said is, that slaves are property.

"Is there any question that, by the law of war, property, both of enemies and friends, may be taken when needed; and is it not needed whenever taking it helps us to hurt the enemy?

"If the Proclamation is not valid in law, it needs no retraction; if it is valid, it cannot be retracted, any more than the dead can be brought to life.

"There was more than a year and a half of trial to suppress the rebellion before the Proclamation was issued, the last one hundred days of which passed under an explicit notice that it was coming unless it was averted by those in revolt returning to their allegiance. The war has certainly progressed as favorably for us since the issue of the Proclamation as before. Some of the commanders of our armies in the field who have given us our most important victories believe that the Emancipation Proclamation policy, and the aid of colored troops, constitute the heaviest blows yet dealt to the rebellion; and that at least one of those important successes could not have been achieved when it was but for the aid of black soldiers.

"Whatever negroes can be got to do as soldiers leaves just so much less for white soldiers to do in saving the Union. But negroes, like other people, act upon notions. Why should they do anything for us if we will do nothing for them? If they stake their lives for us there must be the strongest motive—even the promise of their freedom. And the promise being made must be kept.

"The signs look better. The Father of Waters goes unvexed to the sea. Thanks to the great Northwest for it.

"Nor yet wholly to them. Three hundred miles up they met New England, Empire, Keystone, and Jersey, hewing their way right and left. The sunny South, too, in more colors than one, also lent a hand. On the spot their part of the history was jotted down in black and white. The job was a great national one, and let none be banned who bore an honorable part in it.

"Peace does not appear so distant as it did. I hope it

will soon come, and come to stay; and so come as to be worth keeping in all future time. And then there will be some black men who can remember that they helped Mankind on to this great consummation, while I fear that there will be some white men unable to forget that they have striven to hinder it.

"Still let us be ever sanguine of a speedy final triumph. Let us be quite sober. Let us diligently apply the means, never doubting that a just God in His own good time will give us the rightful results.

"Your friend, A. LINCOLN."

PRESENTATION OF A GOLD MEDAL* TO LIEUTENANT-GENERAL GRANT BY PRESIDENT LINCOLN

Executive Mansion, March 7, 1865.

Lieutenant-General Grant:

In accordance with a joint resolution of Congress approved December 16, 1863, I now have the honor of transmitting and presenting to you, in the name of the people of the United States of America, a copy of said resolutions engrossed on parchment together with the gold medal therein ordered and directed.

Please accept for yourself and all under your command the renewed expression of my gratitude for your and their arduous and well-performed public service.

Your obedient servant,

A. LINCOLN.

* The cost of medal was $6,000.

LETTER TO MRS. GURNEY, WIFE OF EMINENT ENGLISH PREACHER OF THE SOCIETY OF FRIENDS

My Esteemed Friend: I have not forgotten—probably never shall forget—the very impressive occasion when yourself and friends visited me on a Sabbath forenoon, two years ago; nor has your kind letter, written nearly a year later, ever been forgotten.

In all it has been your purpose to strengthen my reliance on God.

I am much indebted to the good Christian people of the country for their constant prayers and consolations, and to no one more than to yourself.

The purposes of the Almighty are perfect, and must prevail, though we erring mortals may fail to accurately perceive them in advance.

We hoped for a happy termination of this terrible war long before this; but God knows best, and has ruled otherwise. We shall yet acknowledge His wisdom, and our own error therein.

Meanwhile we must work earnestly in the best lights He gives us, trusting that so working still conduces to the great ends He ordains. Surely, He intends some great good to follow this mighty convulsion, which no mortal could make, and no mortal could stay.

Your people, the Friends, have had, and are having, a very great trial. On principle and faith, opposed to both war and oppression, they can only practically oppose oppression by war. In this hard dilemma, some have chosen one horn, and some the other.

For those appealing to me on conscientious grounds, I have done, and shall do, the best I could and can, in my own conscience, under my oath to the law. That you believe this I doubt not, and believing it I shall still receive for our country and myself your earnest prayers to our Father in heaven.

Your sincere friend,

A. Lincoln.

LINCOLN'S GREAT SPEECHES

LINCOLN'S GREAT SPEECHES

LINCOLN'S FIRST POLITICAL SPEECH

Mr. Lincoln made his first political speech in 1832, at the age of twenty-three, when he was a candidate for the Illinois Legislature. His opponent had wearied the audience by a long speech, leaving him but a short time in which to present his views. He condensed all he had to say into a few words, as follows:

"Gentlemen, Fellow-Citizens: I presume you know who I am. I am humble Abraham Lincoln. I have been solicited by my friends to become a candidate for the Legislature. My politics can be briefly stated. I am in favor of the Internal Improvement System, and a high Protective Tariff. These are my sentiments and political principles. If elected, I shall be thankful. If not, it will be all the same."

THE PERPETUITY OF OUR FREE INSTITUTIONS

Delivered before the Springfield, Ill., Lyceum, in January, 1837, when twenty-eight years of age. Coming, as he did upon this occasion, before a literary society, Mr. Lincoln's Websterian diction is more observable.

"Ladies and Gentlemen: In the great journal of things happening under the sun, we, the American people, find our account running under date of the nineteenth century of the Christian era. We find ourselves in the peaceful possession of the fairest portion of the earth as regards extent of territory, fertility of soil, and salubrity of climate.

"We find ourselves under the government of a system of political institutions conducing more essentially to the ends of civil and religious liberty than any of which history of former times tells us.

"We, when mounting the stage of existence, found ourselves the legal inheritors of these fundamental blessings. We toiled not in the acquisition or establishment of them; they are a legacy bequeathed to us by a once hardy, brave, and patriotic, but now lamented and departed race, of ancestors.

"Theirs was the task (and nobly did they perform it) to possess themselves, us, of this goodly land, to uprear upon its hills and valleys a political edifice of liberty and equal rights; 'tis ours to transmit these—the former unprofaned by the foot of an intruder, the latter undecayed by the lapse of time and untorn by usurpation—to the generation that fate shall permit the world to know. This task, gratitude to our fathers, justice to ourselves, duty to posterity—all imperatively require us faithfully to perform.

"How, then, shall we perform it? At what point shall we expect the approach of danger? Shall we expect some trans-Atlantic military giant to step the ocean and crush us at a blow?

"Never! All the armies of Europe, Asia and Africa, combined, with all the treasures of the earth (our own excepted) in their military chest, with a Bonaparte for a commander, could not, by force, take a drink from the

Ohio, or make a track on the Blue Ridge, in a trial of a thousand years.

"At what point, then, is this approach of danger to be expected? I answer, if ever it reach us, it must spring up amongst us. It cannot come from abroad. If destruction be our lot, we must ourselves be its author and finisher. As a nation of freemen, we must live through all time or die by suicide.

"I hope I am not over-wary; but, if I am not, there is even now something of ill-omen amongst us. I mean the increasing disregard for law which pervades the country, the disposition to substitute the wild and furious passions in lieu of the sober judgment of courts, and the worse than savage mobs for the executive ministers of justice.

"This disposition is awfully fearful in any community, and that it now exists in ours, though grating to our feelings to admit it, it would be a violation of truth and an insult to deny.

Accounts of outrages committed by mobs form the every-day news of the times. They have pervaded the country from New England to Louisiana; they are neither peculiar to the eternal snows of the former, nor the burning sun of the latter.

"They are not the creatures of climate, neither are they confined to the slave-holding or non-slave-holding States. Alike they spring up among the pleasure-hunting masters of Southern slaves and the order-loving citizens of the land of steady habits. Whatever, then, their cause may be, it is common to the whole country.

"Many great and good men, sufficiently qualified for any task they may undertake, may ever be found, whose ambition would aspire to nothing beyond a seat in Congress, a gubernatorial or presidential chair; but such belong not to the family of the lion, or the tribe of the eagle.

"What! Think you these places would satisfy an Alexander, a Cæsar, or a Napoleon? Never! Towering genius disdains a beaten path. It seeks regions hitherto unexplored.

"It seeks no distinction in adding story to story upon the monuments of fame, erected to the memory of others. It denies that it is glory enough to serve under any chief. It scorns to tread in the footpaths of any predecessor, however illustrious. It thirsts and burns for distinction, and, if possible, it will have it, whether at the expense of emancipating the slaves or enslaving freemen.

"Another reason which once was, but which to the same extent is now no more, has done much in maintaining our institutions thus far. I mean the powerful influence which the interesting scenes of the Revolution had upon the passions of the people, as distinguished from their judgment.

"But these histories are gone. They can be read no more forever. They were a fortress of strength. But what the invading foeman could never do, the silent artillery of time has done,—the levelling of the walls. They were a forest of giant oaks, but the all-resisting hurricane swept over them and left only here and there a lone trunk, despoiled of its verdure, shorn of its foliage, unshading and unshaded, to murmur in a few more gentle breezes and to combat with its mutilated limbs a few more rude storms, then to sink and be no more. They were the pillars of the temple of liberty, and now that they have crumbled away, that temple must fall, unless we, the descendants, supply the places with pillars hewn from the same solid quarry of sober reason.

"Passion has helped us, but can do so no more. It will in future be our enemy.

"Reason—cold, calculating, unimpassioned reason—must furnish all the materials for our support and defense. Let those materials be molded into general intelligence, sound morality, and, in particular, a reverence for the Constitution and the laws; and then our country shall continue to improve, and our nation, revering his name, and permitting no hostile foot to pass or desecrate his resting-place, shall be the first to hear the last trump that shall awaken our Washington.

"Upon these let the proud fabric of freedom rest as the rock of its basis, and as truly as has been said of the only greater institution, 'the gates of hell shall not prevail against it.' "

NATIONAL BANK VS. SUB-TREASURY

Delivered in the Second Presbyterian Church, Springfield, Illinois, and published in the Sangamon Journal, March 6, 1840. The debaters on the question were Messrs. Logan, Baker, Browning and Lincoln, against Douglas, Calhoun, Lamborn and Thomas.

"Fellow-citizens: It is peculiarly embarrassing to me to attempt a continuance of the discussion, on this evening, which has been conducted in this hall on several preceding ones.

"It is so, because on each of these evenings there was a much fuller attendance than now, without any reason for its being so except the greater interest the community feel in the speaker who addressed them then than they do in him who addresses them now.

"I am, indeed, apprehensive that the few who have attended have done so more to spare me mortification than in the hope of being interested in anything I may be able to say.

"This circumstance casts a damp upon my spirits which I am sure I shall be unable to overcome during the evening.

"The subject heretofore and now to be discussed is the sub-treasury scheme of the present administration, as a means of collecting, safe-keeping, transferring and disbursing the revenues of the nation as contrasted with a national bank for the same purpose.

"Mr. Douglas has said that we (the Whigs) have not dared to meet them (the Locos) in argument on this question.

"I protest against this assertion. I say we have again and again during this discussion urged facts and arguments against the sub-treasury which they have neither dared to deny nor attempted to answer.

"But lest some may be led to believe that we really wish to avoid the question, I now propose, in my humble way, to urge these arguments again, at the same time begging the audience to mark well the positions I shall take and the proof I shall offer to sustain them, and that they will not allow Mr. Douglas or his friends to escape the force of them by a round of groundless assertions that we dare not meet them in argument.

"First. It will injuriously affect the community by its operation on the circulating medium.

"Second. It will be a more expensive fiscal agent.

"Third. It will be a less secure depository for the public money.

"Mr. Lamborn insists that the difference between the Van Buren party and the Whigs is, that although the former sometimes err in practice, they are always correct in principle, whereas the latter are wrong in principle; and the better to impress this proposition he uses a figurative expression in these words:

" 'The Democrats are vulnerable in the heel, but they are sound in the heart and head.'

"The first branch of the figure—that the Democrats are vulnerable in the heel—I admit is not merely figurative, but literally true. Who that looks for a moment at their Swartwouts, their Prices, their Harringtons, and their hundreds of others scampering away with the public money to Texas, to Europe, and to every spot on earth where a villain may hope to find refuge from justice, can at all doubt that they are most distressingly affected in their heels with a species of running itch?

"It seems this malady of the heels operates on the sound-headed and honest-hearted creatures very much like the cork leg in the comic song did on its owner, which, when he had once got started on it, the more he tried to stop it the more it would run away.

"At the hazard of wearing this point threadbare, I will relate an anecdote which is too strikingly in point to be omitted:

"A witty Irish soldier who was always boasting of his bravery when no danger was near, who invariably retreated without orders at the first charge of the engagement, being asked by the captain why he did so, replied, 'Captain, I have as brave a heart as Julius Cæsar ever had, but somehow or other, when danger approaches, my cowardly legs will run away with it!'

"So with Mr. Lamborn's party.

"They take the public money into their own hands for the most laudable purposes that wise heads and willing hearts can dictate; but, before they can possibly get it out again, their rascally vulnerable heels will run away with them.

"Mr. Lamborn refers to the late elections in the States, and from the result predicts that every State in the Union will vote for Mr. Van Buren at the next Presidential election.

"Address that argument to cowards and knaves; with the free and the brave it will affect nothing. It may be true; if it must, let it. Many free countries have lost their liberty, and ours may lose hers; but if she shall, be it my proudest plume, not that I was the last to desert, but that I never deserted her.

"I know that the great volcano at Washington, aroused by the civil spirits that reign there, is belching forth the laws of political corruption in a current broad and deep, which is sweeping with frightful velocity over the whole length and breadth of the land, bidding fair to leave unscathed no green spot or living thing; while on its bosom are riding, like demons on the wave of hell, the imps of that evil spirit fiendishly taunting all those who dare resist its destroying course with hopelessness of their efforts; and, knowing this, I cannot deny that all may be swept away. Broken by it, I, too, may be; bow to it, I never will.

"The probability that we may fall in the struggle ought not to deter us from the support of a course we believe to be just. It shall not deter me.

"If ever I feel the soul within me elevate and expand to those dimensions, not wholly unworthy of its Almighty architect, it is when I contemplate the cause of my country deserted by all the world beside, and I standing up boldly alone, hurling defiance at her victorious opposers.

"Here, without contemplating the consequences, before heaven and in the face of the world, I swear eternal fealty to the just cause, as I deem it, of the land of my life, my liberty, and my love.

"And who that thinks with me will not fearlessly adopt that oath that I take? Let none falter who thinks he is right, and we may succeed. But if, after all, we may fail, be it so; we shall still have the proud consolation of saying to our conscience, and to the departed shade of our country's freedom, that the cause approved of our judgment and adored of our hearts in disaster, in chains, in torture, in death, we never faltered in defending."

A GREAT CONGRESSIONAL SPEECH

Abraham Lincoln on the Presidency and general politics. Delivered in the House of Representatives, Washington, D. C., July 27, 1848.

"Mr. Speaker: Our Democratic friends seem to be in great distress because they think our candidate for the Presidency don't suit us. Most of them cannot find out that General Taylor has any principles at all, some, however, have discovered that he has one, but that one is entirely wrong. This one principle is his position on the veto power.

"The gentleman from Tennessee (Mr. Stanton) who has just taken his seat, indeed, has said there is very little if any difference on this question between General Taylor and all the Presidents; and he seems to think it sufficient detraction from General Taylor's position on it, that it has nothing new in it. But all others, whom I have heard speak, assail it furiously.

"A new member from Kentucky (Mr. Clarke), of very considerable ability, was in particular concern about it.

He thought it altogether novel and unprecedented for a President, or a Presidential candidate, to think of approving bills whose Constitutionality may not be entirely clear to his own mind. He thinks the ark of our safety is gone, unless Presidents shall always veto such bills as, in their judgment, may be of doubtful Constitutionality. However clear Congress may be of their authority to pass any particular act, the gentleman from Kentucky thinks the President must veto if he has doubts about it.

"Now, I have neither time nor inclination to argue with the gentleman on the veto power as an original question; but I wish to show that General Taylor, and not he, agrees with the earliest statesmen on this question. When the bill chartering the first Bank of the United States passed Congress, its Constitutionality was questioned; Mr. Madison, then in the House of Representatives, as well as others, opposed it on that ground. General Washington, as President, was called on to approve or reject it. He sought and obtained, on the Constitutional question, the separate written opinion of Jefferson, Hamilton and Edmund Randolph, they then being respectively Secretary of State, Secretary of the Treasury, and Attorney-General. Hamilton's opinion was for the power; while Randolph's and Jefferson's were both against it. Mr. Jefferson, after giving his opinion decidedly against the Constitutionality of that bill, closed his letter with the paragraph I now read:

" 'It must be admitted, however, that unless the President's mind, on a view of everything which is urged for and against this bill, is tolerably clear that it is unauthorized by the Constitution; if the pro and the con hang so even as to balance his judgment, a just respect for the wisdom of the Legislature would naturally decide the balance in favor of their opinion; it is chiefly for cases where they are clearly misled by error, ambition or interest, that the Constitution has placed a check in the negative of the President.

" 'Thomas Jefferson.

" 'February 15, 1791.'

"General Taylor's opinion, as expressed in his Allison letter, is as I now read:

" 'The power given by the veto is a high conservative power; but, in my opinion, should never be exercised, except in cases of clear violation of the Constitution, or manifest haste and want of consideration by Congress.'

"It is here seen that, in Mr. Jefferson's opinion, if on the Constitutionality of any given bill, the President doubts, he is not to veto it, as the gentleman from Kentucky would have him to do, but is to defer to Congress and approve it. And if we compare the opinions of Jefferson and Taylor, as expressed in these paragraphs, we shall find them more exactly alike than we can often find any two expressions having any literal difference. None but interested fault-finders can discover any substantial variation.

"But gentlemen on the other side are unanimously agreed that General Taylor has no other principle. They are in utter darkness as to his opinions on any of the questions of policy which occupy the public attention. But is there any doubt as to what he will do on the prominent questions, if elected? Not the least. It is not possible to know what he will, or would do in every imaginable case; because many questions have passed away, and others doubtless will arise which none of us have yet thought of; but on the prominent questions of currency, tariff, internal improvements, and Wilmot Proviso, General Taylor's course is at least as well defined as is General Cass'. Why, in their eagerness to get at General Taylor, several Democratic members here have desired to know whether, in case of his election, a bankrupt law is to be established. Can they tell us General Cass' opinion on this question? (Some member answered: 'He is against it.') Aye, how do you know he is? There is nothing about it in the platform, or elsewhere, that I have seen. If the gentleman knows anything which I do not, he can show it. But to return: General Taylor, in his Allison letter, says:

" 'Upon the subject of the tariff, the currency, the improvement of our great highways, rivers, lakes, and harbors, the will of the people, as expressed through their Representatives in Congress, ought to be respected and carried out by the Executive.'

"Now, this is the whole matter—in substance it is this: The people say to General Taylor:

" 'If you are elected, shall we have a National Bank?'

"He answers: 'Your will, gentlemen, not mine.'

" 'What about the tariff?'

" 'Say yourselves.'

" 'Shall our rivers and harbors be improved?'

" 'Just as you please. If you desire a bank, an alteration of the tariff, internal improvements, any or all, I will not hinder you. Send up your members to Congress from the various districts, with opinions according to your own, and if they are for these measures, or any of them, I shall have nothing to oppose; if they are not for them, I shall not, by any appliance whatever, attempt to dragoon them into their adoption.'

"Now, can there be any difficulty in understanding

this? To you, Democrats, it may not seem like principle; but surely you cannot fail to perceive the position plainly enough. The distinction between it and the position of your candidate is broad and obvious, and I admit you have a clear right to show it is wrong, if you can; but you have no right to pretend you cannot see it at all. We see it, and to us it appears like principle, and the best sort of principle at that—the principle of allowing the people to do as they please with their own business.

"My friend from Indiana (Mr. C. B. Smith) has aptly asked: 'Are you willing to trust the people?' Some of you answered, substantially: 'We are willing to trust the people; but the President is as much the representative of the people as Congress.' In a certain sense, and to a certain extent, he is the representative of the people. He is elected by them, as well as Congress is. But can he, in the nature of things, know the wants of the people as well as three hundred other men coming from the various localities of the nation? If so, where is the propriety of having a Congress? That the Constitution gives the President a negative on legislation all know; but that this negative should be so combined with platforms and other appliances as to enable him, and in fact, almost compel him, to take the whole of legislation into his own hands, is what we object to—is what General Taylor objects to—and is what constitutes the broad distinction between you and us. To thus transfer legislation is clearly to take it from those who understand with minuteness the interest of the people, and give it to one who does not and cannot so well understand it.

"I understand your idea, that if a Presidential candidate avow his opinion upon a given question, or rather upon all questions, and the people, with full knowledge of this, elect him, they thereby distinctly approve all those opinions. This, though plausible, is a most pernicious deception. By means of it measures are adopted or rejected, contrary to the wishes of the whole of one party, and often nearly half of the other. The process is this: Three, four, or a half-dozen questions are prominent at a given time; the party selects its candidate, and he takes his position on each of these questions. All but one of his positions have already been indorsed at former elections, and his party fully committed to them; but that one is new, and a large portion of them are against it. But what are they to do? The whole are strung together, and they must take all or reject all. They cannot take what they like and leave the rest. What they are already committed to, being the majority, they shut their eyes and gulp the whole. Next election still another is introduced in the same way.

"If we run our eyes along the line of the past, we shall see that almost, if not quite, all the articles of the present Democratic creed have been at first forced upon the party in this very way. And just now, and just so, opposition to internal improvements is to be established if General Cass shall be elected. Almost half the Democrats here are for improvements, but they will vote for Cass, and if he succeeds, their votes will have aided in closing the doors against improvements. Now, this is a process which we think is wrong. We prefer a candidate who, like General Taylor, will allow the people to have their own way regardless of his private opinion; and I should think the internal improvement Democrats at least, ought to prefer such a candidate. He would force nothing on them which they don't want, and he would allow them to have improvements, which their own candidate, if elected, will not.

"Mr. Speaker, I have said that General Taylor's position is as well defined as is that of General Cass. In saying this, I admit I do not certainly know what he would do on the Wilmot Proviso. I am a Northern man, or rather a Western free State man, with a constituency I believe to be, and with personal feelings I know to be, against the extension of slavery. As such, and with what information I have, I hope, and believe, General Taylor, if elected, would not veto the proviso, but I do not know it. Yet, if I knew he would I still would vote for him. I should do so, because in my judgment his election alone can defeat General Cass; and because should slavery thereby go into the territory we now have, just so much will certainly happen by the election of Cass; and in addition, a course of policy leading to new wars, new acquisitions of territory, and still further extension of slavery. One of the two is to be President; which is preferable?

"But there is as much doubt of Cass on improvements as there is of Taylor on the proviso. I have no doubt of General Cass on this question, but I know the Democrats differ among themselves as to his position. My internal improvement colleague (Mr. Wentworth) stated on this floor the other day, that he was satisfied Cass was for improvements, because he had voted for all the bills that he (Mr. W.) had. So far so good. But Mr. Polk vetoed some of these very bills; the Baltimore Convention passed a set of resolutions, among other things, approving these vetoes, and Cass declares in his letter accepting the nomination, that he has carefully read these resolutions, and that he adheres to them as firmly as he approves them cordially. In other words, General Cass voted for the bills, and thinks the President did right to veto them; and his friends here are amiable enough to consider him as being on one side or the other, just as one or the other may correspond with their own respective inclinations.

"My colleague admits that the platform declares against the Constitutionality of a general system of improvements, and that General Cass indorses the platform; but he still thinks General Cass is in favor of some sort of improvements. Well, what are they? As he is against general objects, those he is for must be particular and local. Now, this is taking the subject precisely by the wrong end. Particularity—expending the money of the whole people for an object which will benefit only a portion of them, is the greatest objection to improvements, and has been so held by General Jackson, Mr. Polk, and all others, I believe, till now. But now behold, the objects most general, nearest free from this objection, are to be rejected, while those most liable to it are to be embraced. To return: I cannot help believing that General Cass, when he wrote his letter of acceptance, well understood he was to be claimed by the advocates of both sides of this question, and that he then closed the doors against all further expressions of opinion, purposely to retain the benefits of that double position. His subsequent equivocation at Cleveland, to my mind, proves such to have been the case.

"One word more, and I shall have done with this branch of the subject. You Democrats, and your candidate, in the main, are in favor of laying down, in advance, a platform—a set of party positions, as a unit; and then of enforcing the people, by every sort of appliance, to ratify them, however unpalatable some of them may be. We, and our candidate, are in favor of making Presidential elections and the legislation of the country distinct matters; so that the people can elect whom they please, and afterward legislate just as they please, without any hindrance, save only so much as may guard against infractions of the Constitution, undue haste, and want of consideration.

"The difference between us is as clear as noon-day. That we are right we cannot doubt. We hold the true Republican position. In leaving the people's business in their hands, we cannot be wrong. We are willing, and even anxious, to go to the people on this issue.

"But I suppose I cannot reasonably hope to convince you that we have any principles. The most I can expect is, to assure you that we think we have, and are quite contented with them.

"The other day, one of the gentlemen from Georgia (Mr. Iverson), an eloquent man, and a man of learning, so far as I can judge, not being learned myself, came down upon us astonishingly. He spoke in what the Baltimore American calls the 'scathing and withering style.' At the end of his second severe flash I was struck blind, and found myself feeling with my fingers for an assurance of my continued physical existence. A little of the bone was left, and I gradually revived. He eulogized Mr. Clay in high and beautiful terms, and then declared that we had deserted all our principles, and had turned Henry Clay out, like an old horse, to root. This is terribly severe. It cannot be answered by argument; at least I cannot so answer it.

"I merely wish to ask the gentleman if the Whigs are the only party he can think of who sometimes turn old horses out to root! Is not a certain Martin Van Buren an old horse, which your party turned out to root? and is he not rooting to your discomfort about now? But in not nominating Mr. Clay, we deserted our principles, you say. Ah! in what? Tell us, ye men of principle, what principle we violated? We say you did violate principle in discarding Martin Van Buren, and we can tell you how. You violated the primary, the cardinal, the one great living principle of all Democratic representative government—the principle that the representative is bound to carry out the known will of his constituents.

"A large majority of the Baltimore Convention of 1844 were, by their constituents, instructed to procure Van Buren's nomination if they could. In violation, in utter, glaring contempt of this, you rejected him—rejected him, as the gentleman from New York (Mr. Birdsall), the other day, expressly admitted, for availability—that same 'general availability' which you charge on us, and daily chew over here, as something exceedingly odious and unprincipled.

"But the gentleman from Georgia (Mr. Iverson), gave us a second speech yesterday, all well considered and put down in writing, in which Van Buren was scathed and withered a 'few' for his present position and movements. I can not remember the gentleman's precise language, but I do remember he put Van Buren down, down, till he got him where he was finally to 'sink' and 'rot.'

"By the way, Mr. Speaker, did you know I am a military hero? Yes, sir, in the days of the Black Hawk war I fought, bled, and came away. Speaking of General Cass' career, reminds me of my own. I was not at Stillman's defeat, but I was about as near it as Cass to Hull's surrender; and like him, I saw the place very soon afterward. It is quite certain I did not break my sword, for I had none to break; but I bent a musket pretty badly on one occasion. If Cass broke his sword, the idea is, he broke it in desperation; I bent the musket by accident. If General Cass went in advance of me in picking whortleberries, I guess I surpassed him in charges upon wild onions. If he saw any live, fighting Indians, it was more than I did, but I had a good many bloody struggles with the mosquitoes; and although I never fainted from loss of blood, I can truly say I was often very hungry.

"Mr. Speaker, if I should ever conclude to doff whatever our Democratic friends may suppose there is of black-cockade Federalism about me, and, thereupon, they should take me up as their candidate for the Presidency, I protest they shall not make fun of me as they have of General Cass, by attempting to write me into a military hero.

"While I have General Cass in hand, I wish to say a word about his political principles. As a specimen, I take the record of his progress on the Wilmot Proviso. In the Washington Union, of March 2, 1847, there is a report of the speech of General Cass, made the day before in the Senate, on the Wilmot Proviso, during the delivery of which Mr. Miller, of New Jersey, is reported to have interrupted him as follows, to-wit:

" 'Mr. Miller expressed his great surprise at the change in the sentiments of the Senator from Michigan, who had been regarded as the great champion of freedom in the Northwest, of which he was a distinguished ornament. Last year the Senator from Michigan was understood to be decidedly in favor of the Wilmot Proviso; and, as no reason had been stated for the change, he (Mr. Miller) could not refrain from the expression of his extreme surprise.'

"To this General Cass is reported to have replied as follows, to-wit:

"Mr. Cass said that the course of the Senator from New Jersey was most extraordinary. Last year he (Mr. Cass) should have voted for the proposition had it come up. But circumstances had altogether changed. The honorable Senator then read several passages from the remarks given above, which he had committed to writing in order to refute such a charge as that of the Senator from New Jersey.

"In the 'remarks above committed to writing,' is one numbered 4, as follows, to-wit:

" '4th. Legislation would now be wholly imperative, because no territory hereafter to be acquired can be governed without an act of Congress providing for its government. And such an act, on its passage, would open the whole subject, and leave the Congress, called on to pass it, free to exercise its own discretion, entirely uncontrolled by any declaration found in the statute book.'

"In Niles' Register, vol. 73, page 293, there is a letter of General Cass to A. O. P. Nicholson, of Nashville, Tennessee, dated December 25, 1847, from which the following are correct extracts:

" 'The Wilmot Proviso has been before the country some time. It has been repeatedly discussed in Congress, and by the public press. I am strongly impressed with the opinion that a great change has been going on in the public mind upon this subject—in my own as well as others; and that doubts are resolving themselves into convictions, that the principle it involves should be kept out of the National Legislature, and left to the people of the Confederacy in their respective local governments.

" 'Briefly, then, I am opposed to the exercise of any

jurisdiction by Congress over this matter; and I am in favor of leaving the people of any territory which may be hereafter acquired, the right to regulate it themselves, under the general principles of the Constitution. Because:

" 'I do not see in the Constitution any grant of the requisite power to Congress; and I am not disposed to extend a doubtful precedent beyond its necessity—the establishment of territorial governments when needed—leaving to the inhabitants all the rights compatible with the relations they bear to the Confederation.'

"These extracts show, in 1846, General Cass was for the Proviso at once; that, in March, 1847, he was still for it but not just then; and that, in December, 1847, against it altogether. This is a true index to the whole man. When the question was raised in 1846, he was in a blustering hurry to take ground for it. He sought to be in advance, and to avoid the uninteresting position of a mere follower; but soon he began to see a glimpse of the great Democratic ox-gad waving in his face, and to hear indistinctly a voice saying, 'Back, back, sir; back a little.' He shakes his head and bats his eyes, and blunders back to his position of March, 1847; and still the gad waves and the voice grows more distinct, and sharper still—'Back, sir! back, I say! further back!' and back he goes to the position of December, 1847; at which the gad is still, and the voice soothingly says, 'So! stand still at that.'

"Have no fears, gentlemen, of your candidate, he exactly suits you, and we congratulate you upon it. However much you may be distressed about our candidate you have all cause to be contented and happy with your own. If elected he may not maintain all, or even any of his positions previously taken; but he will be sure to do whatever the party exigency, for the time being, may require;

and that is precisely what you want. He and Van Buren are the same 'manner of men'; and like Van Buren, he will never desert you till you first desert him.

"But I have introduced General Cass' accounts here, chiefly to show the wonderful physical capacities of the man. They show that he not only did the labor of several men at the same time, but that he often did it at several places many hundred miles apart, at the same time. And at eating, too, his capacities are shown to be quite as wonderful. From October, 1821, to May, 1822, he ate ten rations a day in Michigan, ten rations a day here in Washington, and near five dollars' worth a day besides, partly on the road between the two places.

"And then there is an important discovery in his example—the art of being paid for what one eats, instead of having to pay for it. Hereafter, if any nice man shall owe a bill which he cannot pay in any other way, he can just board it out.

"Mr. Speaker, we have all heard of the animal standing in doubt between two stacks of hay, and starving to death; the like of that would never happen to General Cass. Place the stacks a thousand miles apart, he would stand stock-still, midway between them, and eat both at once; and the green grass along the line would be apt to suffer some, too, at the same time. By all means, make him President, gentlemen. He will feed you bounteously—if—if there is any left after he shall have helped himself.

"But as General Taylor is, par excellence, the hero of the Mexican war; and, as you Democrats say we Whigs have always opposed the war, you think it must be very awkward and embarrassing for us to go for General Taylor.

"The declaration that we have always opposed the war

is true or false according as one may understand the term, 'opposing the war.' If to say 'the war was unnecessarily and unconstitutionally commenced, by the President' be opposing the war, then the Whigs have very generally opposed it. Whenever they have spoken at all they have said this; and they have said it on what has appeared good reason to them: The marching of an army into the midst of a peaceful Mexican settlement, frightening the inhabitants away, leaving their growing crops and other property to destruction, to you may appear a perfectly amiable, peaceful, unprovoking procedure; but it does not appear so to us. So to call such an act, to us appears no other than a naked, impudent absurdity; and we speak of it accordingly. But if, when the war had begun, and become the cause of the country, the giving of our money and our blood, in common with yours, was support of the war, then it is not true that we have always opposed the war. With few individual exceptions, you have constantly had our votes here for all the necessary supplies.

"And, more than this, you have had the services, the blood, and the lives of our political brethren in every trial and on every field. The beardless boy and the mature man—the humble and the distinguished, you have had them. Through suffering and death, by disease, and in battle they have endured, and fought, and fallen with you. Clay and Webster each gave a son, never to be returned.

"From the State of my own residence, besides other worthy but less known Whig names, we sent Marshall, Morrison, Baker, and Hardin; they all fought, and one fell, and in the fall of that one, we lost our best Whig man. Nor were the Whigs few in number, or laggard in the day of danger. In that fearful, bloody, breathless struggle at Buena Vista, where each man's hard task was to beat back five foes, or die himself, of the five high officers who perished, four were Whigs.

"In speaking of this, I mean no odious comparison between the lion-hearted Whigs and Democrats who fought there. On other occasions, I doubt not the proportion was different. I wish to do justice to all. I think of all those brave men as Americans, in whose proud fame, as an American, I, too, have a share. Many of them, Whigs and Democrats, are my constituents and personal friends; and I thank them—more than thank them—one and all, for the high, imperishable honor they have conferred on our common State.

"But the distinction between the cause of the President in beginning the war, and the cause of the country after it was begun, is a distinction which you cannot perceive. To you, the President and the country seem to be all one. You are interested to see no distinction between them; and I venture to suggest that possibly your interest blinds you a little.

"We see the distinction, as we think, clearly enough; and our friends, who have fought in the war, have no difficulty in seeing it also. What those who have fallen would say, were they alive and here, of course we can never know; but with those who have returned there is no difficulty.

"Colonel Haskell and Major Gaines, members here, both fought in the war; and one of them underwent extraordinary perils and hardships; still they, like all other Whigs here, vote on the record that the war was unnecessarily and unconstitutionally commenced by the President.

"And even General Taylor himself, the noblest Roman

of them all, has declared that, as a citizen, and particularly as a soldier, it was sufficient for him to know that his country was at war with a foreign nation, to do all in his power to bring it to a speedy and honorable termination, by the most vigorous and energetic operations, without inquiring about its justice, or anything else connected with it.

"Mr. Speaker, let our Democratic friends be comforted with the assurance that we are content with our position, content with our company, and content with our candidate; and that although they, in their generous sympathy, think we ought to be miserable, we really are not, and that they may dismiss the great anxiety they have on our account."

LINCOLN'S TEMPERANCE SPEECH

Originally printed as "An address by Abraham Lincoln, Esq." Delivered before the Springfield Washingtonian Temperance Society, at the Second Presbyterian Church, on the 22d day of February, 1842:

"Although the temperance cause has been in progress for nearly twenty years, it is apparent to all that it is just now being crowned with a degree of success hitherto unparalleled.

"The list of its friends is daily swelled by the addition of fifties, hundreds, and thousands. The cause itself seems suddenly transformed from a cold, abstract theory to a living, breathing, active, and powerful chief thing, going forth 'conquering and to conquer.' The citadels of his great adversary are daily being stormed and dismantled; his temples and his altars, where the rites of his idolatrous worship have long been performed, and where human sacrifices have long been wont to be made, are daily desecrated and deserted. The tramp of the conqueror's fame is sounding from hill to hill, from sea to sea, from land to land, and calling millions to his standard at a blast.

"For this new and splendid success we heartily rejoice. That success is so much greater now than heretofore is doubtless owing to rational causes; and if we would have it continue, we shall do well to enquire what those causes are.

"The warfare heretofore waged against the demon intemperance has, somehow or other, been erroneous. Either the champions engaged or the tactics they have adopted have not been the most proper. These champions, for the most part, have been teachers, lawyers, and hired agents; between these and a mass of mankind there is a want of approachability, if the term be admissible, partial, fatal to their success. They are supposed to have no sympathy of feeling or interest with those very persons whom it is their object to convince and persuade.

"And, again, it is so easy and so common to ascribe motives to men of these classes other than those they profess to act upon. The preacher, it is said, advocates temperance because he is a fanatic, and desires a union of the Church and State; the lawyer, from his pride and vanity of hearing himself speak; and the hired agent, for his salary.

"But when one who has long been known as the victim of intemperance bursts the fetters that have bound him and appears before his neighbors 'clothed, in his right mind,' a redeemed specimen of long lost humanity, and stands up with tears of joy trembling in his eyes to tell the miseries once endured, now to be endured no more forever; of his once naked and starving children, now fed and clad comfortably; of a life long weighed down with woe, weeping, and a broken heart, now restored to health, happiness, and a renewed affection, and how easily it is all done, once resolved to be done; how simple his language; there is a logic and eloquence in it that few with human feelings can resist.

"They cannot say that he desired a union of Church and State, for he is not a church member; they cannot say he is vain of hearing himself speak, for his whole demeanor shows he would gladly avoid speaking at all; they cannot say he speaks for pay, for he receives none. Nor can his sincerity in any way be doubted, or his sympathy for those he would persuade to imitate his example be denied.

"In my judgment it is to the battles of this new class of champions our late success is greatly, perhaps chiefly, owing. But had the old school champions themselves been of the most wise selecting? Was their system of tactics the most judicious? It seems to me it was not.

"Too much denunciation against dram-sellers and dram-drinkers was indulged in. This, I think, was both impolitic, and unjust. It was impolitic, because it is not much in the nature of man to be driven to anything, still less to be driven about that which is exclusively his own business; and least of all, where such driving is to be submitted to at the expense of pecuniary interest, or burning appetite.

"When the dram-seller and drinker were incessantly told, not in the accents of entreaty and persuasion, diffidently addressed by erring men to an erring brother, but in the thundering tones of anathema and denunciation, with which the lordly judge often groups together all the crimes of the felon's life and thrusts them in his face just ere he passes sentence of death upon him, that they were the authors of all the vice and misery and crime in the land; that they were the manufacturers and material of all the thieves and robbers and murderers that infest the earth; that their houses were the workshops of the devil, and that their persons should be shunned by all the good and virtuous as moral pestilences—I say, when they were told all this, and in this way, it is not wonderful that they were slow, very slow, to acknowledge the truth of such denunciation, and to join the ranks of their denouncers in a hue and cry against themselves.

"To have expected them to do otherwise than they did—to have expected them not to meet denunciation with denunciation, crimination with crimination, and anathema with anathema—was to expect a reversal of human nature, which is God's decree and can never be reversed.

"When the conduct of men is designed to be influenced, persuasion, kind, unassuming persuasion, should ever be adopted. It is an old and true maxim that, 'A drop of honey catches more flies than a gallon of gall.' So with men.

"If you would win a man to your cause, first convince him that you are his sincere friend. Therein is the drop of honey that catches his heart; which, do what he will, is the great road to his reason, and which, when once gained, you will find but little trouble in convincing his judgment of the justice of your cause, if indeed, that cause be really a just one. On the contrary, assume to dictate to his judgment, or to command his action, or to mark him as one to be shunned and despised, and he will retreat within himself, close all the avenues to his head and his heart, and though your cause be the naked truth itself, transformed to the heaviest lance, harder than steel, and sharper than steel can be made, and though you throw it with more than herculean force and precision, you shall be no more able to pierce him than to penetrate the hard shell of a tortoise with a rye straw. Such is man, and so must he be understood by those who would lead him, even to his own best interest.

"On this point the Washingtonians greatly excel the temperance advocates of former times. Those whom they desire to convince and persuade are their old friends and companions. They know they are not demons, nor even the worst of men; they know that generally they are kind, generous, and charitable, even beyond the example of the more staid and sober neighbors. They are practical philanthropists; and they glow with a generous and brotherly zeal, that mere theorizers are incapable of feeling. Benevolence and charity possess their heart entirely; and out of the abundance of their heart their tongues give utterance: 'Love through all their actions runs, and all their words are mild'; in this spirit they speak and act, and in the same they are heard and regarded. And when such is the temper of the advocate, and such of the audience, no good cause can be unsuccessful. But I have said that denunciations against dram-sellers and dram-drinkers are unjust as well as impolitic. Let us see.

"I have not inquired at what period of time the use of intoxicating liquors commenced, nor is it important to know. It is sufficient that to all of us who now inhabit the world the practice of drinking them is just as old as the world itself—that is, we have seen the one just as long as we have seen the other. When all of us, who have now reached the years of maturity, first opened our eyes upon the stage of existence, we found intoxicating liquors recognized by everybody, used by everybody, repudiated by nobody. It commonly entered into the first draught of the infant and the last of the dying man.

"From the sideboard of the parson down to the ragged pocket of the homeless loafer, it was constantly found. Physicians prescribed it in this, that, and the other disease; Government provided it for soldiers and sailors; and to have a rolling or a raising, a husking, or hoe-down anywhere about without it, was positively insufferable.

"So, too, it was everywhere a respectable article of manufacture and merchandise. The making of it was regarded as an honorable livelihood, and he who could make most was the most enterprising and respectable. Manufactories of it were everywhere erected, in which all the earthly goods of their owners were invested. Wagons drew it from town to town, boats bore it from clime to clime, and the winds wafted it from nation to nation; and merchants bought and sold it by wholesale and retail with precisely the same feelings on the part of the seller, buyer, and bystander as are felt at the selling and buying of plows, bacon, or any other of the real necessaries of life. Universal public opinion not only tolerated but recognized and adopted its use.

"It is true that even then it was known and acknowledged that many were greatly injured by it; but none seemed to think that the injury arose from the use of a bad thing, but from the use of a very good thing. The victims of it were to be pitied and compassionated, just as are the heirs of consumption and other hereditary diseases. The failing was treated as a misfortune, and not as a crime.

"If, then, what I have been saying is true, is it wonderful that some should think and act now as all thought and acted twenty years ago; and is it just to assail, condemn, or despise them for doing so? The universal sense of mankind, on any subject, is an argument, or at least an influence, not easily overcome.

"The success of the argument in favor of the existence of an overruling Providence mainly depends upon that sense; and men ought not, in justice, to be denounced for yielding to it in any case, or giving it up slowly, especially when they are backed by interest, fixed habits, or burning appetites.

"Another error, as it seems to me, into which the old reformers fell, was the position that all habitual drunkards were utterly incorrigible, and therefore must be turned adrift and damned without remedy, in order that the grace of temperance might abound, to the temperate, then, and to all mankind some hundreds of years thereafter.

"There is in this, something so repugnant to humanity, so uncharitable, so cold-blooded, and feelingless, that it never did, nor never can, enlist the enthusiasm of a popular cause. We could not love the man who taught it—we could not hear him with patience. The heart could not throw open its portals to it; the generous man could not adopt it; it could not mix with his blood. It looked so fiendishly selfish, so like throwing fathers and brothers overboard to lighten the boat for our security, that the noble-minded shrank from the manifest meanness of the thing. And, besides this, the benefits of a reformation to be effected by such a system were too remote in point of time to warmly engage many in its behalf.

"Few can be induced to labor exclusively for posterity, and none will do it enthusiastically. Posterity has done nothing for us; and, theorize on it as we may, practically we shall do very little for it unless we are made to think we are, at the same time, doing something for ourselves.

"What an ignorance of human nature does it exhibit to ask or expect a whole community to rise up and labor for the temporal happiness of others, after themselves shall be consigned to the dust, when a majority of this community take no pains whatever to secure their own eternal welfare! Great distance in either time or space has wonderful power to lull and render quiescent the human mind. Pleasures to be enjoyed, or pains to be endured, after we shall be dead and gone, are but little regarded, even in our own cases, and much less in the case of others.

"Still, in addition to this, there is something so ludicrous in promises of good or threats of evil a great way off, as to render the whole subject with which they are connected easily turned to ridicule. 'Better lay down that spade you're stealing, Paddy—if you don't you'll pay for it at the day of judgment.' 'By the powers, if ye'll credit me so long, I'll take another jist.'

"By the Washingtonians this system of consigning the habitual drunkard to hopeless ruin is repudiated. They adopt a more enlarged philanthropy. They go for present as well as for future good. They labor for all now living, as well as hereafter to live. They teach hope to all —despair to none. As applying to their cause, they deny the doctrine of unpardonable sin. As in Christianity, it is taught, so in this they teach:

> " 'While the lamp holds out to burn,
> The vilest sinner may return.'

"And, that which is a matter of most profound congratulation, is the fact that they, by experiment upon experiment, and example upon example, prove the maxim to be no less true in the one case than in the other. On every hand we behold those who but yesterday were the chief of sinners, now the chief apostles of the cause. Drunken devils are cast out by ones, by sevens, by legions, and their unfortunate victims, like the poor possessed who was redeemed from his long and lonely wandering in the tomb, are publishing to the ends of the earth how great things have been done for them.

"To these new champions and this new system of tactics our late success is mainly owing, and to them we must mainly look for the final consummation. The ball is now rolling gloriously on, and none are so able as they to increase its speed and its bulk, to add to its momentum and magnitude. Even though unlearned in letters, for this task none are so well educated. To fit them for this work they have been taught in the true school. They have been in that gulf from which they would teach others the means of escape. They have passed that prison wall which others have long declared impassable, and who that has not, shall dare to weigh opinions with them as to the mode of passing?

"But if it be true, as I have insisted, that those who have suffered by intemperance personally and have reformed are the most powerful and efficient instruments to push the reformation to ultimate success, it does not follow that those who have not suffered have no part left them to perform. Whether or not the world would be vastly benefited by total and final banishment from it of all intoxicating drinks seems to me not now an open question. Three-fourths of mankind confess the affirmative with their tongues, and I believe all the rest acknowledge it in their hearts.

"Ought any, then, to refuse their aid in doing what the good of the whole demands? Shall he who cannot do much be for that reason excused if he do nothing? 'But,' says one, 'what good can I do by signing the pledge? I never drink, even without signing.' This question has already been asked and answered more than a million times. Let it be answered once more. For the man, suddenly or in any other way, to break off from the use of drams, who has indulged in them for a long course of years, and until his appetite has grown ten or a hundred fold stronger and more craving than any natural appetite can be, requires a most powerful moral effort. In such an undertaking, he needs every moral support and influence that can possibly be brought to his aid and thrown around him. And not only so, but every moral prop should be taken from whatever argument might rise in his mind to lure him to his backsliding. When he casts his eyes around him, he should be able to see all that he respects, all that he admires, all that he loves, kindly and anxiously pointing him onward and none beckoning him back to his former miserable 'wallowing in the mire.'

"But it is said by some that men will think and act for themselves; that none will disuse spirits or anything else because his neighbors do; and that moral influence is not that powerful engine contended for. Let us examine this. Let me ask the man who would maintain this position most stiffly what compensation he will accept to go to church some Sunday and sit during the sermon with his wife's bonnet upon his head? Not a trifle, I'll venture. And why not? There would be nothing irreligious in it, nothing immoral, nothing uncomfortable—then, why not? Is it not because there would be something egregiously unfashionable in it? Then it is the influence of fashion; and what is the influence of fashion but the influence that other people's actions have on our own actions—the strong inclination each of us feels to do as we see all of our neighbors do? Nor is the influence of fashion confined to any particular thing or class of things. It is just as strong on one subject as another. Let us make it as unfashionable to withhold our names from the temperance pledge as for husbands to wear their wives' bonnets to church, and the instances will be just as rare in the one case as the other.

" 'But,' some say, 'we are no drunkards, and we shall not acknowledge ourselves such by joining a reformed drunkards' society, whatever our influence might be.' Surely, no Christian will adhere to this objection.

"If they believe as they profess, that Omnipotence condescended to take on Himself the form of sinful man, and as such to die an ignominious death for their sakes, surely they will not refuse submission to the infinitely lesser condescension for the temporal and perhaps eternal salvation of a large, erring, and unfortunate class of their fellow creatures. Nor is the condescension very great. In my judgment such of us as have never fallen victims have been spared more from the absence of appetites than from any mental or moral superiority over those who have. Indeed, I believe, if we take habitual drunkards as a class, their heads and their hearts will bear an advantageous comparison with those of any other class.

"There seems to have ever been a proneness in the

brilliant and warm-blooded to fall into this vice—the demon of intemperance ever seems to have delighted in sucking the blood of genius and generosity. What one of us but can call to mind some relative more promising in youth than all his fellows, who has fallen a sacrifice to his rapacity? He ever seems to have gone forth like the Egyptian angel of death, commissioned to slay, if not the first, the fairest born of every family. Shall he now be arrested in his desolating career? In that arrest all can give aid that will, and who shall be excused that can and will not? Far around as human breath has ever blown, he keeps our fathers, our brothers, our sons, and our friends prostrate in the chains of moral death. To all the living everywhere we cry: 'Come, sound the moral trump, that these may rise and stand up an exceeding great army.' 'Come from the four winds, O Breath! and breathe upon these slain, that they may live.' If the relative grandeur of revolutions shall be estimated by the great amount of human misery they alleviate, and the small amount they inflict, then, indeed, will this be the grandest the world has ever seen.

"Of our political revolution of 1776, we are all justly proud. It has given us a degree of political freedom far exceeding that of any other nation of the earth. In it the world has found a solution of the long-mooted problem as to the capability of man to govern himself. In it was the germ that has vegetated, and still is to grow and expand into the universal liberty of mankind.

"But with all these glorious results, past, present, and to come, it has its evils. It breathed forth famine, swam in blood, and rode in fire; and long, and long after, the orphan's cry and the widow's wail continued to break the sad silence that ensued. These were the price, the inevitable price, paid for the blessing it bought.

"Turn now to the temperance revolution. In it we shall find a stronger bondage broken, a viler slavery manumitted, a greater tyrant deposed—in it, more of want supplied, more disease healed, more sorrow assuaged. By it, no orphans starving, no widows weeping; by it, none wounded in feeling, none injured in interest. Even the dram-maker and seller will have glided into other occupations so gradually as never to have felt the change, and will stand ready to join all others in the universal song of gladness. And what a noble ally this to the cause of political feeling; with such an aid, its march cannot fail to be on and on, till every son of earth shall drink in rich fruition the sorrow-quenching draughts of perfect liberty! Happy day, when, all appetite controlled, all passion subdued, all matter subjugated, mind, all-conquering mind, shall live and move, the monarch of the world! Glorious consummation! Hail, fall of fury! Reign of reason, all hail!

"And when the victory shall be complete—when there shall be neither a slave nor a drunkard on the earth—how proud the title of that land, which may truly claim to be the birthplace and the cradle of both those revolutions that shall have ended in that victory! How nobly distinguished that people who shall have planted and nurtured to maturity both the political and moral freedom of their species!

"This is the one hundred and tenth anniversary of the birthday of Washington. We are met to celebrate this day. Washington is the mightiest name of earth—long since mightiest in the cause of civil liberty, still mightiest in moral reformation. On that name a eulogy is expected. It cannot be. To add brightness to the sun or glory to the name of Washington is alike impossible. Let none attempt it. In solemn awe pronounce the name, and in its naked, deathless splendor leave it shining on."

THE BALLOT VS. THE BULLET

Delivered to a delegation at Springfield, Ill., that proposed to visit Kansas Territory in the physical defense of freedom, in 1856. Hon. W. H. Herndon was in this delegation:

"Friends: I agree with you in Providence. I believe in the providence of most men, the largest purse, and the longest cannon. You are in the minority—in a sad minority; and you can't hope to succeed, reasoning from all human experience. You would rebel against the Government, and redden your hands in the blood of your countrymen. If you are in the minority, as you are, you can't succeed. I say again and again, against the Government, with a great majority of its best citizens backing it, and when they have the most men, the longest purse, and the biggest cannon, you can't succeed. If you have the majority, as some say you have, you can succeed with the ballot, throwing away the bullet. You can peaceably then redeem the Government, and preserve the liberties of mankind, through your votes and voice and moral influence.

"Let there be peace. In a democracy, where a majority rule by the ballot through the forms of law, these physical rebellions and bloody resistances are radically wrong, unconstitutional, and are treason. Better bear the ills you have than to fly to those you know not of. Our own Declaration of Independence says that the government long established, for trivial causes should not be resisted. Revolutionize through the ballot-box, and restore the government once more to the affections and hearts of men, by making it express, as it was intended to do, the highest spirit of justice and liberty.

"Your attempt, if there be such, to resist the laws of Kansas by force, is criminal and wicked; and all your feeble attempts will be follies, and end in bringing sorrow on your heads, and ruin the cause you would freely die to preserve."

LINCOLN'S FIRST SPEECH IN THE SENATORIAL CAMPAIGN—"THE HOUSE-DIVIDED-AGAINST-ITSELF" SPEECH

Delivered at Springfield, Ill., June 6, 1858, before the Republican State Convention. It is known as one of Lincoln's greatest speeches:

"Gentlemen of the Convention: If we could first know where we are, and whither we are tending, we could better judge what to do, and how to do it. We are now far into the fifth year, since a policy was initiated with the avowed object and confident promise of putting an end to slavery agitation. Under the operation of that policy, that agitation has not ceased, but has constantly augmented. In my opinion, it will not cease until a crisis shall have been reached and passed. 'A house divided against itself cannot stand.' I believe this Government cannot endure permanently half slave and half free. I do not expect the Union to be dissolved—I do not expect the house to fall—but I do expect it will cease to be divided. It will become all one thing or all the other. Either the opponents of slavery will arrest the further spread of it, and place it where the public mind shall rest in the belief that it is in the course of ultimate extinction; or its advocates will push it forward, till it shall become alike lawful in all the States, old as well as new—North as well as South.

"Have we no tendency to the latter condition?

"Let any one who doubts, carefully contemplate that now almost complete legal combination—piece of machinery, so to speak—compounded of the Nebraska doctrine and the Dred Scott decision. Let him consider not only what work the machinery is adapted to do, and how well adapted; but also let him study the history of its construction, and trace, if he can, or rather fail, if he can, to trace the evidence of design and concert of action among its chief architects, from the beginning.

A FEW IMPORTANT FACTS

"The year of 1844 found slavery excluded from more than half the States by State Constitutions, and from most of the national territory by Congressional prohibition. Four days later commenced the struggle which ended in repealing that Congressional prohibition. This opened all the national territory to slavery, and was the first point gained.

"But, so far, Congress had acted; and an indorsement by the people, real or apparent, was indispensable, to save the point already gained, and give chance for more.

"This necessity had not been overlooked; but had been

provided for, as well as might be, in the notable argument of 'squatter sovereignty,' otherwise called 'sacred right of self-government,' which latter phrase, though expressive of the only rightful basis of any government, was so perverted in this attempted use of it as to amount to just this:

"That, if any one man chose to enslave another, no third man shall be allowed to object. That argument was incorporated into the Nebraska bill itself, in the language which follows:

" 'It being the true intent and meaning of this act not to legislate slavery into any Territory or State, nor to exclude it therefrom; but to leave the people thereof perfectly free to form and regulate their domestic institutions in their own way, subject only to the Constitution of the United States.'

"Then opened the roar of loose declamation in favor of 'squatter sovereignty,' and 'sacred right of self-government.' 'But,' said opposition members, 'let us amend the bill so as to expressly declare that the people of the territory may exclude slavery.' 'Not we,' said the friends of the measure; and down they voted the amendment.

"While the Nebraska bill was passing through Congress, a law case involving the question of a negro's freedom, by reason of his owner having voluntarily taken him first into a free State and then into a Territory covered by the Congressional prohibition, and held him as a slave for a long time in each, was passing through the United States District Court for the district of Missouri; and both Nebraska bill and law suit were brought to a decision in the same month of May, 1854. The negro's name was 'Dred Scott,' which name now designates the decision finally made in the case.

"Before the then next Presidential election, the case came to, and was argued in, the Supreme Court of the United States, but the decision of it was deferred until after the election.

"Still, before the election, Mr. Trumbull, on the floor of the Senate, requested the leading advocate of the Nebraska Bill to state his opinion whether the people of a territory can constitutionally exclude slavery from their limits; and the latter answers: 'That is a question for the Supreme Court.'

"The election came. Mr. Buchanan was elected, and the endorsement, such as it was, secured. That was the second point gained. The endorsement, however, fell short of a clear popular majority of nearly four hundred thousand votes, and so, perhaps, was not overwhelmingly reliable and satisfactory. The out-going President, in the last annual message, as impressively as possible echoed back upon the people the weight and authority of the endorsement. The Supreme Court met again; did not announce their decision, but ordered a re-argument. The next Presidential inauguration came, and still no decision of the court; but the incoming President in his inaugural address fervently exhorted the people to abide by the forthcoming decision, whatever it might be. Then, in a few days, came the decision.

"The reputed author of the Nebraska bill finds an early occasion to make a speech at this capital indorsing the Dred Scott decision, and vehemently denouncing all opposition to it. The new President, too, seizes the early occasion of the Sillman letter to indorse and strongly commend that decision, and to express his astonishment that any different view had ever been entertained.

VOTING IT UP OR DOWN

"At length a squabble sprang up between the President and the author of the Nebraska bill, on the mere question of fact, whether the Lecompton Constitution was or was not, in any just sense, made by the people of Kansas; and in that quarrel the latter declares that all he wants is a fair vote for the people, and that he cares not whether slavery be voted down or up. I do not understand his declaration that he cares not whether slavery be voted down or up to be intended by him other than an apt definition of the policy he would impress upon the public mind—the principle for which he declares he has suffered so much, and is ready to suffer to the end. And well may he cling to that principle. If he has any parental feelings, well may he cling to it. That principle is the only shred left of his original Nebraska doctrine.

"Under the Dred Scott decision squatter sovereignty squatted out of existence, tumbled down like temporary scaffolding—like the mould at the foundry, served through one blast and fell back into loose sand—helped to carry an election and then was kicked to the winds. His late joint struggle with the Republicans, against the Lecompton Constitution, involves nothing of the original Nebraska doctrine. That struggle was made on a point—the right of the people to make their own constitution—upon which he and the Republicans have never differed.

"The several points of the Dred Scott decision, in connection with Senator Douglas' care-not policy, constitute the piece of machinery, in its present state of advancement. This was the third point gained.

WORKING POINTS

"The working points of that machinery are:

"First. That no negro slave, imported as such from Africa, and no descendant of such slave, can ever be a citizen of any State, in the sense of that term as used in the Constitution of the United States. This point is made in order to deprive the negro, in every possible event, of the benefit of that provision of the United States Constitution which declares that 'the citizens of each State shall be entitled to all the privileges and immunities of citizens in the several States.'

"Secondly. That, 'subject to the Constitution of the United States,' neither Congress nor a Territorial Legislature can exclude slavery from any United States territory. This point is made in order that individual men may fill up the Territories with slaves, without danger of losing them as property, and thus to enhance the chances of permanency to the institution through all the future.

"Thirdly. That, whether the holding of the negro in actual slavery in a free State makes him free, as against the holder, the United States courts will not decide, but will leave to be decided by the courts of any slave State the negro may be forced into by the master.

"This point is made, not to be pressed immediately, but, if acquiesced in for a while, and apparently indorsed by the people at an election, then, to sustain the logical conclusion that what Dred Scott's master might lawfully do with Dred Scott, in the free State of Illinois, every other master may lawfully do with any other one, or one thousand slaves, in any other free State.

"Auxiliary to all this, and working hand in hand with

it, the Nebraska doctrine, or what is left of it, is to educate and mold public opinion, at least northern public opinion, not to care whether slavery is voted down or up. This shows exactly where we now are; and partially, also, whither we are tending.

A STRING OF HISTORICAL FACTS

"It will throw additional light on the matter, to go back and run the mind over the string of historical facts already stated. Several things will now appear less dark and mysterious than they did when they were transpiring. The people were to be left 'perfectly free,' subject only to the Constitution.

"What the Constitution had to do with it outsiders could not then see. Plainly enough, now, it was an exactly fitted niche, for the Dred Scott decision to afterward come in, and declare the perfect freedom of the people to be just no freedom at all. Why was the amendment, expressly declaring the right of the people voted down? Plain enough now; the adoption of it would have spoiled the niche for the Dred Scott decision. Why was the court decision held up. Why even a Senator's individual opinion withheld, till after the presidential election? Plainly enough now; the speaking out then would have damaged the perfectly free argument upon which the election was to be carried. Why the outgoing President's felicitation on the indorsement? Why the delay of a re-argument? Why the incoming President's advance exhortation in favor of the decision? These things look like the cautious patting and petting of a spirited horse preparatory to mounting him, when it is dreaded that he may give the rider a fall. And why the hasty after-indorsement of the decision by the President and others?

"We cannot absolutely know that all these exact adaptations are the result of preconcert. But when we see a lot of framed timbers, different portions of which we know have been gotten out at different times and places by different workmen—Stephen, Franklin, Roger, and James, for instance—and when we see these timbers joined together, and see they exactly make the frame of a house or mill, all the tenons and mortices exactly adapted, and all the lengths and proportions of the different pieces exactly adapted to their respective places, and not a piece too many or too few—not omitting even scaffolding—or, if a single piece be lacking, we see the place in the frame, exactly fitted and prepared yet to bring such a piece in—in such a case, we find it impossible not to believe that Stephen and Franklin and Roger and James all understood one another from the beginning, and all worked upon a common plan or draft drawn before the first blow was struck.

POWER OF A STATE

"It should not be overlooked, that, by the Nebraska bill, the people of a State as well as Territory, were to be left 'perfectly free, subject only to the Constitution.' Why mention a State? They were legislating for Territories, and not for or about States.

"Certainly, the people of a State are, or ought to be, subject to the Constitution of the United States; but why is mention of this lugged into this merely territorial law? But why are the people of a Territory and the people of a State therein lumped together, and their relation to the

Constitution therein treated as being precisely the same? While the opinions of the court, by Chief Justice Taney, in the Dred Scott case, and the separate opinions of all the concurring judges, expressly declare that the Constitution of the United States neither permits Congress nor a Territorial Legislature to exclude slavery from any United States Territory, they all omit to declare whether or not the same Constitution permits a State, or the people of a State, to exclude it.

"Possibly, that is a mere omission; but who can be quite sure, if McLean or Curtis had sought to get into the opinion a declaration of unlimited power in the people of a State to exclude slavery from their limits, just as Chase and Mace sought to get such declaration, in behalf of the people of a Territory, into the Nebraska bill; I ask, who can be quite sure that it would not have been voted down in the one case as it has been in the other?

"The nearest approach to the point of declaring the power of a State over slavery, is made by Judge Nelson. He approaches it more than once, using the precise idea and almost the language, too, of the Nebraska act. On one occasion, his exact language is, 'Except in cases where the power is restrained by the Constitution of the United States, the law of the State is supreme over the subject of slavery within its jurisdiction.'

"In what cases the power of the States is so restrained by the United States Constitution is left an open question, precisely as the same question as to the restraint on the power of the Territories was left open in the Nebraska act. Put this and that together, and we have another nice little niche, which we may, ere long, see filled with another Supreme Court decision, declaring that the Constitution of the United States does not permit a State to exclude slavery from its limits. And this may especially be expected if the doctrine of 'care not whether slavery be voted down or up' shall gain upon the public mind sufficiently to give promise that such a decision can be maintained when made.

"Such a decision is all that slavery now lacks of being alike lawful in all the States. Welcome or unwelcome, such a decision is probably coming, and will soon be upon us, unless the power of the present political dynasty shall be met and overthrown. We shall lie down pleasantly dreaming that the people of Missouri are on the very verge of making their State free, and we shall wake to the reality instead, that the Supreme Court has made Illinois a slave State. To meet and overthrow the power of that dynasty, is the work now before all those who would prevent that consummation. That is what we have to do. How can we best do it?

"A LIVING DOG IS BETTER THAN A DEAD LION."

"There are those who denounce us openly to their friends, and yet whisper us softly that Senator Douglas is the aptest instrument there is with which to effect that object. They wish us to infer all from the fact that he now has a little quarrel with the present head of the dynasty; and that he has regularly voted with us on a single point, upon which he and we have never differed. They remind us that he is a great man, and that the largest of us are very small ones. Let this be granted. But 'a living dog is better than a dead lion,' for this work, is, at least, a caged and toothless one. How can he oppose the advances of slavery? He don't care anything about it. His avowed mission is impressing the 'public heart' to care nothing about it.

"A leading Douglas Democratic newspaper, treating upon this subject, thinks Douglas's superior talent will be needed to resist the revival of the African slave trade. Does Douglas believe an effort to revive that trade is approaching? He has not said so. Does he really think so? But, if it is, how can he resist it? For years he has labored to prove it a sacred right of white men to take negro slaves into the new Territories. Can he possibly show that it is less a sacred right to buy them where they can be bought the cheapest? And unquestionably they can be bought cheaper in Africa than Virginia. He has done all in his power to reduce the whole question of slavery to one of a mere right of property; and, as such, how can he oppose the foreign slave trade—how can he refuse that trade in that 'property' shall be 'perfectly free'—unless he does it as a protection to the home production? And as the home producers will probably not ask the protection, he will be wholly without a ground of opposition.

DOUGLAS IS NOT WITH US

"Senator Douglas holds, we know, that a man may rightfully be wiser to-day than he was yesterday—that he may rightfully change when he finds himself wrong. But can we, for that reason, run ahead; and infer that he will make any particular change of which he himself has given no intimation? Can we safely base our actions upon any such vague reference? Now, as ever, I wish not to misrepresent Judge Douglas's position, question his motives, or do aught that can be personally offensive to him. Whenever, if ever, he and we can come together on principle so that our cause may have assistance from his great ability, I hope to have interposed no adventitious obstacle. But, clearly, he is not now with us—he does not pretend to be—he does not pretend ever to be.

BUT WE SHALL NOT FAIL; THE VICTORY IS SURE

"Our cause, then, must be intrusted to, and conducted by, its own undoubted friends—those whose hands are free, whose hearts are in the work—who do care for the result. Two years ago the Republicans of the nation mustered over thirteen thousand strong. We did this under the single impulse of resistance to a common danger, with every external circumstance against us. Of strange, discordant, and even hostile elements, we gathered from the four winds, and formed and fought the battle through, under the constant hot fire of a disciplined, proud and pampered enemy. Did we brave all then, to falter now? now, when that same enemy is wavering, dissevered and belligerent? The result is not doubtful. We shall not fail—if we stand firm, we shall not fail. Wise counsels may accelerate, or mistakes delay it, but, sooner or later, the victory is sure to come."

DOUGLAS'S SEVEN QUESTIONS—LINCOLN'S POSITION DEFINED ON THE QUESTIONS OF THE DAY.

Delivered at Freeport, Ill., July, 1858:

"Ladies and Gentlemen: On Saturday last, Judge Douglas and myself first met in public discussion. He spoke an hour, I an hour and a half, and he replied for half an hour. The order is now reversed. I am to speak an hour, he an hour and a half, and then I am to reply for half an hour. I propose to devote myself during the first hour to the scope of what was brought within the range of his half-hour's speech at Ottawa. Of course, there was brought within the scope of that half-hour's speech something of his own opening speech. In the course of that opening argument Judge Douglas proposed to me seven different interrogatories.

"In my speech of an hour and a half, I attended to some other parts of his speech; and incidentally, as I thought, answered one of the interrogatories then. I then distinctly intimated to him that I would answer the rest of his interrogatories on condition only that he should agree to answer as many for me. He made no intimation at the time of the proposition, nor did he in his reply allude at all to that suggestion of mine. I do him no injustice in saying that he occupied at least half of his reply in dealing with me as though I had refused to answer his interrogatories. I now propose that I will answer any of the interrogatories upon condition that he will answer questions from me not exceeding the same number. I give him an opportunity to respond. I now say that I will answer his interrogatories whether he answers mine or not [applause]; and that after I have done so, I will propound mine to him. [Applause.]

"I have supposed myself, since the organization of the Republican party at Bloomington, in May, 1856, bound as a party man to the platform of the party, then and since. If in any interrogatories which I shall answer I go beyond the scope of what is in these platforms, it will be perceived that no one is responsible but myself.

"Having said this much, I will take up the Judge's interrogatories as I find them in the Chicago Times, and answer them seriatim. In order that there may be no mistake about it, I have copied the interrogatories in writing, and also my answers to them. The first one of these interrogatories is in these words:

"Q. 1. 'I desire to know whether Lincoln to-day stands, as he did in 1854, in favor of the unconditional repeal of the Fugitive Slave Law?'

"A. I do not now, nor never did, stand in favor of the unconditional repeal of the Fugitive Slave Law.

"Q. 2. 'I desire him to answer whether he stands pledged to-day, as he did in 1854, against any more slave States coming into the Union, even if the people want them?'

"A. I do not now, nor never did, stand pledged against the admission of any more slave States into the Union.

"Q. 3. 'I want to know whether he stands pledged against the admission of a new State into the Union with such a Constitution as the people of that State may see fit to make?'

"A. I do not stand against the admission of a new State into the Union with such a Constitution as the people of that State may see fit to make.

"Q. 4. 'I want to know whether he stands to-day pledged to the abolition of slavery in the District of Columbia?'

"A. I do not stand to-day pledged to the abolition of slavery in the District of Columbia.

"Q. 5. 'I desire him to answer whether he stands pledged to the prohibition of the slave trade between the different States?'

"A. I do not stand pledged to the prohibition of the slave trade between the different States.

"Q. 6. 'I desire to know whether he stands pledged to prohibit slavery in all the Territories of the United

States, North as well as South of the Missouri Compromise line?'

"A. I am impliedly, if not expressedly, pledged to a belief in the right and duty of Congress to prohibit slavery in the United States Territories. [Great applause.]

"Q. 7. 'I desire to know whether he is opposed to the acquisition of any new territory unless slavery is first prohibited therein?'

"A. I am not generally opposed to honest acquisition of territory; and, in any given case, I would or would not oppose such acquisition, accordingly as I might think such acquisition would or would not agitate the slavery question among ourselves.

"Now, my friends, it will be perceived upon examination of these questions and answers, that so far I have only answered that I was not pledged to that or the other thing. The Judge has not framed his interrogatories to ask me anything more than this, and I have answered in strict accordance with his interrogatories, and have answered truly that I am not pledged at all upon any of the points to which I have answered. But I am not disposed to hang upon the exact form of his interrogatory. I am rather disposed to take up at least some of these questions, and state what I really think upon them.

LINCOLN'S POSITION MORE FULLY DEFINED

"As to the first one, in regard to the Fugitive Slave Law, I have never hesitated to say, that I think, under the Constitution of the United States, the people of the Southern States are entitled to a Congressional slave law.

Having said that, I have nothing to say in regard to the existing Fugitive Slave Law, farther than that I think it should have been framed so as to be free from some of the objections that pertain to it, without lessening its efficiency. And, inasmuch, as we are not in agitation upon the general question of slavery.

"In regard to the other question, of whether I am pledged to the admission of any more slave States into the Union, I state to you frankly that I would be exceedingly sorry ever to be put in a position of having to pass upon that question. I should be exceedingly glad to know that there would never be another slave State admitted into the Union; but I must add, that if slavery shall be kept out of the Territories during the Territorial existence of any one given Territory, and then the people shall, having a fair chance in a clear field, when they come to adopt the Constitution, do such an extraordinary thing as to adopt the Constitution, uninfluenced by the actual presence of the institution among them, I see no alternative, if we own the country, but to admit them into the Union. [Applause.]

"The third interrogatory is answered by the answer to the second, it being, as I conceive, the same as the second.

"The fourth one is in regard to the abolition of slavery in the District of Columbia. In relation to that, I have my mind very distinctly made up. I should be exceedingly glad to see slavery abolished in the District of Columbia. I believe that Congress has Constitutional power to abolish it. Yet, as a member of Congress, I should not with my present views be in favor of endeavoring to abolish slavery in the District of Columbia, unless it would be upon these conditions. First, that the abolition should be gradual; second, that it should be on a vote of the majority of qualified voters of the District; and third, that a compensation should be made to unwilling owners. With these three conditions, I confess that I would be exceedingly glad to see Congress abolish slavery in the District of Columbia, and, in the language of Henry Clay, 'sweep from our Capital that foul blot upon our Nation.'

"In regard to the fifth interrogatory, I must say, that, as to the question of abolition of the slave trade between the different States, I can truly answer, as I have, that I am pledged to nothing about it. It is a subject to which I have not given that mature consideration that would make me feel authorized to state a position so as to hold myself entirely bound by it. In other words, that question has never been prominently enough before me to induce me to investigate whether we really have the constitutional power to do it. I could investigate if I had sufficient time to bring myself to a conclusion upon that subject; but I have not done so, and I say so frankly to you here, and to Judge Douglas. I must say, however, that if I should be of the opinion that Congress does possess the Constitutional power to abolish slave trading among the different States, I should not still be in favor of that power unless upon some conservative principle, as I conceive it, akin to what I have said in relation to the abolition of slavery in the District of Columbia.

"My answer as to whether I desire that slavery should be prohibited in all Territories of the United States, is full and explicit within itself, and cannot be made clearer by any comment of mine. So I suppose, in regard to the question whether I am opposed to the acquisition of any more territory unless slavery is abolished, is such that

I could add nothing by way of illustration, or making myself better understood, than the answer which I have placed in writing.

"Now, in all this, the Judge has me, and he has me on the record. I suppose he had flattered himself that I was really entertaining one set of opinions for one place and another set for another place—that I was afraid to say at one time what I uttered at another. What I am saying here I suppose I say to a vast audience in the State of Illinois, and I believe I am saying that which, if it would be offensive to any persons and render them enemies to myself, would be offensive to persons in this audience."

A HUMOROUS SPEECH—LINCOLN IN THE BLACK HAWK WAR.

The friends of General Cass, when that gentleman was a candidate for the Presidency, endeavored to endow him with a military reputation. Mr. Lincoln, at that time a representative in Congress, delivered a speech before the House, which, in its allusion to Mr. Cass, was exquisitely sarcastic and irresistibly humorous:

"By the way, Mr. Speaker," said Mr. Lincoln, "do you know I am a military hero? Yes, sir, in the days of the Black Hawk War, I fought, bled, and came away. Speaking of General Cass's career reminds me of my own. I was not at Stillman's defeat, but I was about as near it as Cass to Hull's surrender; and like him I saw the place very soon afterwards. It is quite certain I did not break my sword, for I had none to break, but I bent my musket pretty badly on one occasion. . . . If General Cass went in advance of me picking whortleberries, I guess I surpassed him in charging upon the wild onion. If he saw any live, fighting Indians, it was more than I did, but I had a good many bloody struggles with the mosquitoes, and although I never fainted from loss of blood, I can truly say that I was often very hungry."

Mr. Lincoln concluded by saying that if he ever turned Democrat and should run for the Presidency, he hoped they would not make fun of him by attempting to make him a military hero!

JOINT DEBATE BETWEEN MR. DOUGLAS AND MR. LINCOLN.

First Joint Debate at Ottawa, August 21, 1858.

MR. DOUGLAS'S SPEECH.

"Ladies and Gentlemen: I appear before you to-day for the purpose of discussing the leading political topics which now agitate the public mind.

"By an arrangement between Mr. Lincoln and myself, we are present here to-day for the purpose of having a joint discussion, as the representatives of the two great parties of the State and Union, upon the principles in issue between these parties; and this vast concourse of people shows the deep feeling which pervades the public mind in regard to the questions dividing us.

"Prior to 1854 this country was divided into two great political parties known as the Whig and Democratic parties. Both were national and patriotic, advocated principles that were universal in their application.

"An old-line Whig could proclaim his principles in

Louisiana and Massachusetts alike. Whig principles had no boundary sectional line—they were not limited by the Ohio River, nor by the Potomac, nor by the line of the free and slave States, but applied and were proclaimed wherever the Constitution ruled, or the American flag waved over the American soil. So it was, and so it is with the great Democratic party, which, from the days of Jefferson until this period, has proved itself to be the historic party of this nation.

"While the Whig and Democratic parties differed in regard to a bank, the tariff distribution, the specie circular and the sub-treasury, they agreed on the great slavery question, which now agitates the Union.

"I say that the Whig party and the Democratic party agreed on this slavery question, while they differed on those matters of expediency to which I have referred.

"The Whig party and the Democratic party adopted the Compromise measures of 1850 as the basis of a proper and just solution of the slavery question in all its forms.

"Clay was the great leader, with Webster on his right and Cass on his left, and sustained by the patriots in the Whig and Democratic ranks, who had devised and enacted the Compromise measure of 1850.

"In 1851 the Whig Party and the Democratic party united in Illinois in adopting resolutions indorsing and approving the principles of the Compromise measure of 1850 as the proper adjustment of that question.

"In 1852, when the Whig party assembled in convention in Baltimore for the purpose of nominating a candidate for the Presidency, the first thing it did was to declare the Compromise measure of 1850, in substance and in principle, a suitable adjustment of that question. [Applause.] My friends, silence will be more acceptable to me in the discussion of these questions than applause. I desire to address myself to your judgment, your understanding, and your consciences, and not to your passion or your enthusiasm.

"When the Democratic Convention assembled in Baltimore in the same year, for the purpose of nominating a Democratic candidate for the Presidency, it also adopted the Compromise measure of 1850 as the basis of Democratic action. Thus you see, that up to 1853-54, the Whig party and the Democratic party both stood on the same platform with regard to the slavery question. That platform was the right of the people of each State and each Territory to decide their local and domestic institutions for themselves, subject only to the Federal Constitution. During the session of Congress of 1853-54, I introduced into the Senate of the United States a bill to organize the Territories of Kansas and Nebraska on that principle which had been adopted in the Compromise measure of 1850, approved by the Whig party and the Democratic party in Illinois in 1851, and endorsed by the Whig party and the Democratic party in National Convention in 1852. In order that there might be no misunderstanding in relation to the principle involved in the Kansas and Nebraska bill, I put forth the true intent and meaning of the act in these words: 'It is the true intent and meaning of this act not to legislate slavery into any State or Territory, or to exclude it therefrom, but to leave the people perfectly free to form and regulate their domestic institutions in their own way, subject to the Federal Constitution.'

"Thus, you see, that in 1854, when the Kansas and Nebraska bill was brought into Congress for the purpose of carrying over the principles which both parties had up to that time endorsed and approved, there had been no division in this country in regard to that principle except the opposition of the Abolitionists. In the House of Representatives of the Illinois Legislature, upon a resolution asserting that principle, every Whig and every Democrat in the House voted in the affirmative, and only four men voted against it, and those four were old-line Abolitionists.

"In 1854, Mr. Abraham Lincoln and Mr. Trumbull entered into an arrangement, one with the other, and each with his respective friends, to dissolve the old Whig party on the one hand, and to dissolve the old Democratic party on the other, and to connect the members of both into an abolition party, under the name and disguise of the Republican party.

"The terms of that arrangement between Mr. Lincoln and Mr. Trumbull have been published to the world by Mr. Lincoln's special friend, H. Matheny, Esq., and they were that Lincoln should have Shields' place in the United States Senate, which was then about to become vacant, and that Mr. Trumbull would have my seat when my term expired.

"Lincoln went to work to abolish the old Whig party all over the State, pretending that he was then as good a Whig as ever; and Trumbull went to work in his part of the State preaching abolitionism in its milder and lighter form, and trying to abolitionize the Democratic party and bring old Democrats handcuffed and bound hand and foot into the abolition camp.

"In the pursuance of this arrangement, the parties met at Springfield in October, 1854, and proclaimed their new platform.

"Lincoln was to bring into the abolition camp the

old-line Whigs, and transfer them over to Giddings, Chase, Fred Douglass, and Parson Lovejoy, who were ready to receive them and christen them in their new party faith. He laid down on that occasion a platform for their new Republican party, which was to be thus constructed. I have their resolutions of the State Convention then held, which was the First mass State Convention ever held in Illinois by the Black Republican party, and I now hold them in my hands, and will read a part of them, and cause the others to be printed. Here are the most important and material resolutions of this abolition platform: [Reading]. Now, Gentlemen, your Black Republicans have cheered every one of those propositions, and yet I venture to say that you cannot get Mr. Lincoln to come out and say that he is now in favor of each one of them.

"That these propositions, one and all, constitute the platform of the Black Republican party of this day, I have no doubt; and when you were not aware for what purpose I was reading them, your Black Republicans cheered them as good Black Republican doctrines.

"My object in reading these resolutions, was to put the question to Abraham Lincoln this day, whether he now stands and will stand by each article in that creed, and carry it out.

"I desire to know whether Mr. Lincoln to-day stands as he did in 1854, in favor of unconditional repeal of the Fugitive Slave Law.

"I desire him to answer whether he stands pledged today, as he did in 1854, against the admission of any more slave States into the Union, even if the people want them. I want to know whether he stands to-day pledged to the abolition of slavery in the District of Columbia. I desire him to answer whether he stands pledged to the prohibition of the slave trade between the different States.

"I desire to know whether he stands pledged to prohibit slavery in all the Territories of the United States, North as well as South of the Missouri Compromise line.

"I desire him to answer whether he is opposed to the acquisition of any more territory unless slavery is prohibited therein. I want his answers to these questions. Your affirmative cheers in favor of the abolition platform are not satisfactory. I ask Abraham Lincoln to answer these questions in order that when I trot him down to lower Egypt I may put the same questions to him.

"My principles are the same everywhere.

"I can proclaim them alike in the North, the South, the East, and the West. My principles will apply whereever the constitution prevails and the American flag waves. I desire to know whether Mr. Lincoln's principles will bear transplanting from Ottawa to Jonesboro? I put these questions to him to-day distinctly, and ask an answer. I have a right to an answer, for I quote from the platform of the Republican party, made by himself and others at the time that party was formed, and the bargain made by Lincoln to dissolve and kill the old Whig party and transfer its members bound hand and foot to the abolition party, under the direction of Giddings and Fred Douglass.

"In the remarks I have made on this platform, and the position of Mr. Lincoln upon it, I mean nothing personally disrespectful or unkind to the gentleman. I have known him for nearly twenty-five years. There were many points of sympathy between us when we first got acquainted.

"We were both comparatively boys, and both struggling with poverty in a strange land.

"I was a schoolteacher in the town of Winchester, and he a flourishing grocery-keeper in the town of Salem.

"He was more successful in his occupation than I was in mine, and hence more fortunate in this world's goods.

"Lincoln is one of those peculiar men who perform with admirable skill everything which they undertake.

"I made as good a schoolteacher as I possibly could, and when a cabinetmaker I made a good bedstead and tables, although my old boss said I succeeded better with bureaus and secretaries than with anything else; but I believe that Lincoln was always more successful in business than I, for his business enabled him to get into the Legislature.

"I met him there, however, and had a sympathy with him, because of the up-hill struggle we both had in life.

"He was then just as good at telling an anecdote as now. He could beat any of the boys wrestling, or running a foot race, in pitching quoits, or tossing a copper; could ruin more liquor than all the boys in the town together, and the dignity and impartiality with which he presided at a horse race or fist fight, excited the admiration and won the praise of everybody that was present and participated. I sympathized with him, because he was struggling with difficulties, and so was I.

"Mr. Lincoln served with me in the Legislature in 1836, when we both retired and he subsided; or became submerged, and he was lost sight of as a public man for several years.

"In 1846, when Wilmot introduced his celebrated proviso, and the abolition tornado swept over the country, Lincoln again turned up as a member of Congress from the Sangamon District. I was then in the Senate of the United States, and was glad to welcome my old friend and companion. While in Congress he distinguished himself by his opposition to the Mexican War, taking the side of the common enemy against his own country; and when he returned home he found that the indignation of the people followed him everywhere, and he was again submerged or obliged to retire into private life, forgotten by his former friends.

"He came up again in 1854, just in time to make this Abolition or Black Republican platform, in company with Giddings, Lovejoy, Chase, and Fred Douglass, for the Republican party to stand upon.

"Trumbull, too, was one of our own contemporaries. He was born and raised in old Connecticut, was bred a Federalist, but removing to Georgia turned nullifier, when nullification was popular, and as soon as he disposed of his clocks and wound up his business, migrated to Illinois, turned politician, and became noted as the author of the scheme to repudiate a large portion of the State debt of Illinois, which, if successful, would have brought infamy and disgrace upon the fair escutcheon of our glorious State. The odium attached to that measure consigned him to oblivion for a time. I helped to do it. I walked to a public meeting in the hall of the House of Representatives, and replied to his repudiating speeches, and resolutions were carried over his head denouncing repudiation, and asserting the moral and legal obligation of Illinois to pay every dollar of the debt she owed and every bond that bore her seal.

"Trumbull's malignity has followed me since I thus defeated his nefarious schemes. These two men, having formed this combination to abolitionize the old Whig party and the old Democratic party, and put themselves into the Senate of the United States, in pursuance of their bargain are now carrying out that arrangement.

"Matheny states that Trumbull broke faith; that the bargain was, that Lincoln should be the Senator in Shields' place, and Trumbull was to wait for mine; and the story goes, that Trumbull cheated Lincoln, having control of four or five abolitionized Democrats who were holding over in the Senate; he would not let them vote for Lincoln, which obliged the rest of the Abolitionists to support him in order to secure an abolition Senator. There are a number of authorities for the truth of this besides Matheny, and I suppose that even Mr. Lincoln will not deny it.

"Mr. Lincoln demands that he shall have the place intended for Mr. Trumbull, as Trumbull cheated him, and got his, and Trumbull is stumping the State traducing me for the purpose of securing the position for Lincoln, in order to quiet him. It was in consequence of this arrangement that the Republican Convention was impaneled to instruct for Lincoln and nobody else, and it was on this account that they passed resolutions that he was their first, their last, and their only choice. Archy Williams was nowhere, Browning was nobody, Wentworth was not to be considered; they had no man in the Republican party for the place except Lincoln, for the reason that he demanded that they should carry out the arrangements. Having formed this new party for the benefit of deserters from Whiggery, and deserters from Democracy, and having laid down the abolition platform which I have read, Lincoln now takes his stand and proclaims his abolition doctrine.

"Let me read a part of them. In his speech at Springfield to the Convention, which nominated him for the Senate, he said: [Reads extracts.] [Applause and "good."] I am delighted to hear you Black Republicans say "good." I have no doubt that doctrine expresses your sentiments, and I will prove to you now, if you will listen to me, that it is revolutionary and destructive of the existence of this Government.

"Mr. Lincoln, in the extract from which I have read, says that the Government cannot endure permanently by the same principles and in the same relative condition in which our fathers made it. Why can it not exist divided into free and slave States? Washington, Jefferson, Franklin, Madison, Hamilton, Jay, and the great men of that day, made this Government divided into free States and slave States, and left each State perfectly free to do as it pleased on the subject of slavery. Why can it not exist on the same principles on which our fathers made it? They knew when they framed the Constitution that in a country as wide and broad as this, with such a variety of climate, productions and interest, the people necessarily required different laws and institutions in different localities.

"They knew that the laws and regulations which would suit the granite hills of New Hampshire would be unsuited to the rice plantations of South Carolina, and they, therefore, provided that each State should retain its own Legislature and its own sovereignty, with the full and complete power to do as it pleased within its own limits, in all that was local and not national.

"One of the reserved rights of the States was the right to regulate the relations between master and servant on the slavery question.

"At the time the Constitution was framed, there were

thirteen States in the Union, twelve of which were slave-holding States, and one a free State. Suppose this doctrine of uniformity preached by Mr. Lincoln, that the States should all be free or all slave, had prevailed, and what would have been the result? Of course, the twelve slave-holding States would have overruled the one free State, and slavery would have been fastened by a Constitutional provision on every inch of the American Republic, instead of being left as our fathers wisely left it, to each State to decide for itself.

"Here I assent that uniformity in the local laws and institutions of the different States is neither possible nor desirable.

"If uniformity had been adopted when the Government was established, it must inevitably have been the uniformity of slavery everywhere, or else the uniformity of negro citizenship and negro equality everywhere. We are told by Lincoln, that he is utterly opposed to the Dred Scott decision, and will not submit to it, for the reason that he says it deprives the negro of the rights and privileges of citizenship.

"That is the first and main reason which he assigns for the warfare on the Supreme Court of the United States and its decision.

"I ask you, are you in favor of conferring upon the negro the rights and privileges of citizenship? Do you desire to strike out of our State Constitution that clause which keeps slaves and free negroes out of the State, and allow the free negroes to flow in, and cover your prairies with black settlements?

"Do you desire to turn this beautiful State into a free negro colony, in order that when Missouri abolishes slavery she can send one hundred thousand emancipated slaves into Illinois, to become citizens and voters on an equality with ourselves?

"If you desire negro citizenship, if you desire them to vote on an equality with yourselves, and to make them eligible to office, to serve on juries and to adjudge our rights, then support Mr. Lincoln and the Black Republican party, who are in favor of the citizenship of the negro.

"For one, I am opposed to negro citizenship in any and every form. I believe this Government was made on the white basis.

"I believe it was made by white men, for the benefit of white men and their posterity forever, and I am in favor of conferring citizenship to white men, men of European birth and descent, instead of conferring it upon negroes, Indians, and other inferior races.

"Mr. Lincoln, following the example and lead of all the little abolition orators, who go around and lecture in the basements of schools and churches, read from the Declaration of Independence, that all men are created equal, and then asks, how can you deprive a negro of that equality which God and the Declaration of Independence award to him? He and they maintain that negro equality is guaranteed by the laws of God, and that it is asserted in the Declaration of Independence.

"If they think so, of course, they have a right to say so, and so vote. I do not question Mr. Lincoln's conscientious belief that the negro was made his equal, and hence is his brother, but for my own part, I do not regard the negro as my equal, and positively deny that he is my brother or any kin to me whatever. Lincoln has evidently learned by heart Parson Lovejoy's catechism. He can repeat as well as Farnsworth, and he is worthy of a medal from Father

Giddings and Fred Douglass for his abolitionism. He holds that the negro was born his equal and yours, and that he was endowed with equality by the Almighty, and that no human law can deprive him of these rights which were guaranteed to him by the Supreme Ruler of the Universe. Now, I do not believe that the Almighty ever intended the negro to be the equal of the white man. If he did, he has been a long time demonstrating the fact. For thousands of years the negro has been a race upon the earth, and during all that time, in all latitudes and climates, wherever he has wandered or been taken, he has been inferior to the race which he has there met. He belongs to an inferior race, and must always occupy an inferior position.

"I do not hold that because the negro is our inferior that therefore he ought to be a slave. By no means can such a conclusion be drawn from what I have said. On the contrary, I hold that humanity and Christianity both require that the negro shall have and enjoy every right, every privilege, and every immunity consistent with the safety of the society in which he lives.

"On that point, I presume, there can be no diversity of opinion.

"You and I are bound to extend to our inferior and dependent beings every right, every privilege, every facility and immunity consistent with the public good.

"The question then arises, what rights and privileges are consistent with the public good?

"This is a question which each State and each Territory must decide for itself—Illinois has decided it for herself. We have provided that the negro shall not be a slave, and we have also provided that he shall not be a citizen, but we protect him in his civil rights, in his life, his person, and his property, only depriving him of all political rights whatsoever, and refusing to put him on an equality with the white man.

"That policy of Illinois is satisfactory to the Democratic party and to me, and if it were to the Republicans, there would be no question upon the subject.

"But the Republicans say he ought to be made a citizen, and when he becomes a citizen, he becomes your equal, with all your rights and privileges.

"They assert the Dred Scott decision to be monstrous because it denies that the negro is or can be a citizen under the Constitution.

"Now, I hold that Illinois has a right to abolish and prohibit slavery, as she did, and I hold that Kentucky has the same right to continue and protect slavery that Illinois had to abolish it. I hold that New York had as much right to abolish slavery as Virginia has to continue it, and that each and every State of this Union is a sovereign power, with the right to do as it pleases on this question of slavery, and upon all its domestic institutions.

"Slavery is not the only question that comes up in this controversy. There is a far more important one to you, and that is, what shall be done with the free negro?

"We have settled the slavery question, so far as we are concerned; we have prohibited it in Illinois forever, and in doing so, I think we have done wisely, and there is no man in the State who would be more strenuous in his opposition to the introduction of slavery than I would; but when we have settled it for ourselves, we have exhausted all our power over that subject. We have done our whole duty, and can do no more.

"We must leave each and every other State to decide

for itself the same question. In relation to the policy to be pursued toward the free negroes, we have said that they shall not vote; whilst Maine, on the other hand, has said that they shall vote. Maine is a sovereign State, and has the power to regulate the qualifications of voters within her limits. I would never consent to confer the right of voting and of citizenship upon a negro, but still I am not going to quarrel with Maine for differing with me in opinion. Let Maine take care of her own negroes and fix the qualifications of her own voters to suit herself, without interfering with Illinois, and Illinois will not interfere with Maine. So with the State of New York. She allows the negro to vote provided he owns two hundred and fifty dollars' worth of property, but not otherwise.

"While I should not make any distinction, whatever, between a negro who held property and one who did not, yet, if the sovereign State of New York chooses to make that distinction, it is her business and not mine, and I will not quarrel with her for it. She can do as she pleases on this question if she minds her own business, and we will do the same thing.

"Now, my friends, if we will only act conscientiously and rigidly upon this great question of popular sovereignty, which guarantees to each State and Territory the right to do as it pleases on all things local, and domestic, instead of Congress interfering, we will continue at peace one with another.

"Why should Illinois be at war with Missouri, or Kentucky with Ohio, or Virginia with New York, merely because their institutions differ. They knew that the North and the South, having different climates, productions and interests, required different institutions.

"This doctrine of Mr. Lincoln's, of uniformity among the institutions of the different States, is a new doctrine never dreamed of by Washington, Madison, or the framers of this Government. Mr. Lincoln and the Republican party set themselves up as wiser than these men who made the Government, which has flourished for seventy years under the principle of popular sovereignty, recognizing the right of each State to do as it pleased. Under that principle we have grown to a nation of about thirty millions of people. We have crossed the Alleghany Mountains, and filled up the whole Northwest, turning the prairie into a garden, and building up churches and schools, thus spreading civilization and Christianity where before there was nothing but savage barbarism. Under that principle we have become, from a feeble nation, the most powerful on the face of the earth, and if we only adhere to that principle, we can go forward increasing in territory, in power, in strength, and in glory until the Republic of America shall be the North Star that shall guide the friends of freedom throughout the civilized world.

"And why can we not adhere to the great principle of self-government, upon which our institutions were originally based? I believe that the new doctrine preached by Mr. Lincoln and his party will dissolve the Union if it succeeds.

"They are trying to array all the Northern States in one body against the South, to excite a sectional war between the free States and the slave States, in order that one or the other may be driven to the wall.

"I am told that my time is out. Mr. Lincoln will now address you for an hour and a half, and I will then occupy a half hour in replying to him."

MR. LINCOLN'S REPLY.

"My Fellow-Citizens: When a man hears himself somewhat misrepresented, it provokes him—at least I find it so with myself, but when misrepresentation becomes very gross and palpable, it is more apt to amuse me.

"The first thing I see fit to notice is the fact that Judge Douglas alleges, after running through the history of the old Democratic and the old Whig parties, that Judge Trumbull and myself made arrangement in 1854, by which I was to have the place of General Shields in the United States Senate, and Judge Trumbull was to have the place of Judge Douglas.

"Now, all that I have to say upon that subject is, that I think no man, not even Judge Douglas, can prove this, because it is not true. I have no doubt he is conscientious in saying it. As to those resolutions that he took such a length of time to read, as being the platform of the Republican party in 1854, I say, I never had anything to do with them.

"I believe this is true about those resolutions: There was a call for a convention to form a Republican party at Springfield, and I think that my friend, Mr. Lovejoy, who is here upon this stand, had a hand in it. I think this is true, and I think, if he will remember accurately, he will be able to recollect that he tried to get me into it, and I would not go in.

"I believe that it is also true that I went away from Springfield when the Convention was in session to attend court in Tazewell County. It is true that they did place my name, though without authority, upon the Committee, and afterward wrote me to attend the meeting of the Committee, but I refused to do so, and I never had anything to do with that organization. This is the plain truth about all that matter of the resolution.

"Now, about that story that Judge Douglas tells of Trumbull bargaining to sell out the old Democratic party, and Lincoln agreeing to sell out the old Whig party, I have the means of knowing about that that Judge Douglas cannot have, and I know there is no substance to it whatever. Yet I have no doubt he is 'conscientious' about it. I know that after Mr. Lovejoy got into the Legislature that winter, he complained of me that I had told all the old Whigs of his district that the old Whig party was good enough for them, and some of them voted against him because I told them so. Now, I have no means of totally disproving such charges as this which the Judge makes.

"A man cannot prove a negative, but he has a right to claim that when a man makes an affirmative charge, he must offer some proof to show the truth of what he says. I certainly cannot introduce testimony to show the negative about things, but I have a right to claim that if a man says he knows a thing, then he must show how he knows it. I always have a right to claim this, and it is not satisfactory to me that he may be conscientious on the subject.

"Now, gentlemen, I hate to waste my time on such things, but in regard to that general abolition tilt that Judge Douglas makes, when he says that I was engaged at that time in selling out and abolitionizing the old Whig party, I hope you will permit me to read a part of a printed speech that I made then at Peoria, which will show altogether a different view of the position I took in that contest of 1854:

" 'This is the repeal of the Missouri Compromise. The

foregoing history may not be precisely accurate in every particular, but I presume it is sufficiently so for all the uses I shall attempt to make of it, and in it we have before us the chief material enabling us to correctly judge whether the repeal of the Missouri Compromise is right or wrong. I think, and shall try to show, that it is wrong; wrong in its direct effects, letting slavery into Kansas and Nebraska, and wrong in its prospective principle, allowing it to spread to every other part of the wide world, where men can be found inclined to take it. This declared indifference, but, as I must think, covert zeal, for the spread of slavery, I cannot but hate. I hate it because of the monstrous injustice of slavery itself—I hate it because it deprives our Republican example of its just influence in the world—enables the enemies of free institutions, with plausibility, to taunt us as hypocrites—causes the real friends of freedom to doubt our sincerity, and especially because it forces so many really good men amongst ourselves into open war with the very fundamental principles of civil liberty—criticising the Declaration of Independence, and insisting that there is no right principle of action but self-interest.

" 'Before proceeding, let me say, I think I have no prejudice against the Southern people. They are just what we would be in their situation. If slavery did not exist among them, they would not introduce it; if it did now exist among us, we should not instantly give it up. This I believe of the masses, north and south. Doubtless there are individuals on both sides who would not hold the slaves under any circumstances, and others who would gladly introduce slavery anew, if it were out of existence.

" 'We know that some Southern men do free their slaves, go north and become tip-top Abolitionists, while some northern ones go south and become most cruel slave masters.

" 'When Southern people tell us they are no more responsible for the origin of slavery than we, I acknowledge the fact. When it is said that the institution exists and that it is very difficult to get rid of it in any satisfactory way, I can understand and appreciate the saying. I surely will not blame them for not doing what I should not know how to do myself. If all earthly powers were given me, I should not know what to do as to the existing institution.

" 'My first impulse would be to free all the slaves and send them to Liberia—to their own native land. But a moment's reflection would convince me that whatever of high hope (as I think there is) there may be in this, in the long run, its sudden execution is impossible.

" 'If they were all landed there in a day, they would all perish there in the next ten days—and there are not surplus shipping and surplus money enough in the world to carry them there in many times ten days. What then? Free them all, and keep them among us as underlings? Is it quite certain that this betters their condition? I think I would not hold them in slavery at any rate, yet the point is not clear enough to me to denounce people upon. What next? Free them, and make them politically and socially our equals? My own feelings will not admit of this; and if mine would, we well know that the great mass of white people will not. Whether this feeling accords with justice and sound judgment is not the sole question, if, indeed, it is any part of it. A universal feeling, whether well or ill founded, cannot be safely disregarded. We cannot, then, make them equals. It does seem to me that systems of gradual emancipation might be adopted; but for their tardiness, I will not undertake to judge our brethren of the South; they remind us of their Constitutional rights, I acknowledge them, not grudgingly, but fully and fairly, and I would give them any legislation for the reclaiming of their fugitives, which should not, in its stringency, be more likely to carry a free man into slavery than our ordinary criminal laws are to hang an innocent one.

" 'But all this, to my judgment, furnishes no more excuse for permitting slavery to go into our own free territory, than it would for revising the African slave-trade by law. The law which forbids the bringing of slaves from Africa, and that which has so long forbid the taking of them to Nebraska, can hardly be distinguished on any moral principle; and the repeal of the former could find quite as plausible excuses as that of the latter.'

"I have reason to know that Judge Douglas knows that I said this; I think he has the answer here to one of his questions he puts to me; I do not mean to allow him to catechise me unless he pays me back in kind. I will not answer questions one after another, unless he reciprocates, but as he has made this inquiry, and I have answered it before, he has got it without my getting anything in return. He has got my answer on the Fugitive Slave Law.

"Now, gentlemen, I don't want to read at any greater length, but this is the true complexion of all I have ever said in regard to the institution of slavery and the black race.

"This is the whole of it, and anything that argues me into his idea of perfect social and political equality with the negro is but a specious and fantastic arrangement of words by which men can prove a horsechestnut to be a chestnut horse. I will say here, while upon this subject, that I have no purpose, directly or indirectly, to interfere with the institution of slavery in the States where it exists. I believe I have no lawful right to do so; I have no purpose to introduce political and social equality between the white and black races. There is a physical difference between the two, which, in my judgment, will probably forever forbid their living together upon the footing of perfect equality, and, inasmuch as it becomes a necessity that there must be a difference, I, as well as Judge Douglas, am in favor of the race to which I belong having the superior position.

"I have never said anything to the contrary, but I hold that, notwithstanding all this, there is no reason in the world why the negro is not entitled to all the natural rights enumerated in the Declaration of Independence, the right to life, liberty, and the pursuit of happiness. I hold that he is as much entitled to these as the white man. I agree with Judge Douglas, he is not my equal in any respect, certainly not in color, perhaps not in moral or intellectual endowments, but in the right to eat the bread, without the leave of anybody else, which his own hand earns, he is my equal and the equal of Judge Douglas, and the equal of any living man.

"Now, I pass on to consider one or two more of these little follies. The Judge is woefully at fault about his early friend Lincoln being a grocery-keeper. I don't know as it would be a great sin, if I had been, but he is mistaken. Lincoln never kept a grocery anywhere in the world; it is true that Lincoln did work the latter part of one winter in a little still-house up at the head of the hollow. And so, I think, my friend, the Judge, is equally at fault when he charges me at the time when I was in Congress of having opposed our soldiers who were fighting in the Mexican War. The Judge did not make his charge very distinctly, but I can tell you how you can prove it, by referring to the record. You remember I was an old Whig, and whenever the Democratic party tried to get me to vote that the war had been righteously made by the President, I would not do it, but whenever they asked for money or land warrants, or anything to pay the soldiers there, during all that time, I gave the same vote that Judge Douglas did. You can think as you please as to whether that was consistent. Such is the truth, and the Judge has the right to make all he can out of it. But when he, by a general statement, conveys the idea that I withheld supplies from the soldiers, he is, to say the least, grossly and altogether mistaken, as a consultation of the records will prove to him.

"As I have not used up so much of my time as I had supposed, I will dwell a little longer upon one or two of these minor topics upon which the Judge has spoken. He has read from my speech in Springfield, in which I said that 'a house divided against itself cannot stand.' Does the Judge say it can stand? I don't know whether he does or not. The Judge does not seem to be attending to me just now, but I would like to know if it is his opinion that a house divided against itself can stand. If he does, then there is a question of veracity, not between him and me, but between the Judge and an authority of a somewhat higher character.

"Now, my friends, I ask your attention to this matter for the purpose of saying something seriously. I know that the Judge may readily enough agree with me that the maxim which was put forth by the Savior is true, but he may allege that I misapply it; and the Judge has a right to urge that, in my application, I do misapply it, and then

I have a right to show that I do not misapply it. When he undertakes to say that because I think this nation, so far as the question is concerned, will all become one thing or all the other, I am in favor of bringing about a dead uniformity in the various States in all their institutions, he argues erroneously. The great variety of the local institutions in the States, springing from differences in the soil, differences in the face of the country, and in the climate, are bonds of union. They do not make a house divided against itself, but they make a house united.

"If they produce in one section of the country what is called for by the wants of another section, and this other section can supply the wants of the first, they are not matters of discord, but bonds of union, true bonds of union. But can this question of slavery be considered as among these varieties in the institutions of the country? I leave it to you to say whether in the history of our Government this institution of slavery has not always failed to be a bond of union, and, on the contrary, been an apple of discord, and an element of division in the house.

"I ask you to consider whether, so long as the moral constitution of men's minds shall continue to be the same, after this generation and assemblage shall sink into the grave, and another race shall arise, with the same moral and intellectual development we have, whether, if that institution is standing in the irritating position in which it now is, it will not continue an element of division? If so, then I have a right to say that, in regard to this question, the Union is a house divided against itself; and when the Judge reminds me that I have often said to him that the institution of slavery has existed for eighty years in some States, and yet it does not exist in some others, I agree to the fact, and I account for it by looking at the position in which our fathers originally placed it,—restricting it from the new Territories where it had not gone, and legislating to cut off its source by the abrogation of the slave-dealer, thus putting the seal of legislation against its spread.

"The public mind did rest in the belief that it was in the course of ultimate extinction. But lately, I think—and in this I charge nothing on the Judge's motives—lately, I think that he, and those acting with him, have placed that institution on a new basis, which looks to the perpetuity and nationalization of slavery. And while it is placed upon this new basis, I say, and have said, that I believe we shall not have peace upon the question until the opponents of slavery arrest the further spread of it, and place it where the public mind shall rest in the belief that it is in the course of ultimate extinction; or, on the other hand, that its advocates will push it forward until it shall become alike lawful in all the States, old as well as new, North as well as South.

"Now, I believe if we could arrest the spread, and place it where Washington and Jefferson and Madison placed it, it would be in the course of ultimate extinction. The crisis would be past, and the institution might be left alone for a hundred years, if it should live so long in the States where it exists, yet it would be going out of existence in the way best for both the black and the white races.

"[A voice—'Then do you repudiate Popular Sovereignty?'] What is Popular Sovereignty? Is it the right of the people to have slavery or not have it, as they see fit, in the Territories? I will state—and I have an able man to match me—my understanding is that Popular Sovereignty, as now applied to the question of slavery, does allow the people of a Territory to have slavery if they want to, but allows them not to have it if they do not want it. I do not mean that if this vast concourse of people were in a Territory of the United States, any one of them would be obliged to have a slave if he did not want one; but I do say that, as I understand the Dred Scott decision, if any one man wants slaves, all the rest have no way of keeping that one man from holding them.

"When I made my speech at Springfield, of which the Judge complains and from which he quotes, I really was not thinking of the things which he ascribes to me at all. I had no thought in the world that I was doing anything to bring about a war between the free and slave States.

"I had no thought in the world that I was doing anything to bring about a political and social equality of the black and white races.

"It never occurred to me that I was doing anything or favoring anything to reduce to a dead uniformity all the local institutions of the various States.

"But I must say, in all fairness to him, if he thinks I am doing something that leads to these bad results, it is none the better that I did not mean it.

"It is just as fatal to the country, if I had any influence in producing it, whether I intended to or not.

"But can it be true, that placing this institution upon the original basis—the basis upon which our fathers placed it—can have any tendency to set the Northern and Southern States at war with one another, or that it can have any tendency to make the people of Vermont raise sugarcane, because they raise it in Louisiana, or that it can compel the people of Illinois to cut pine logs on the Grand Prairie, where they will not grow, because they cut pine logs in Maine, where they do grow? The Judge says this is a new principle started in regard to this question. Does the Judge claim that he is working on the plan of the founders of Government?

"I think he says in some of his speeches—indeed, I have one here now—that he saw evidence of a policy to allow slavery to be south of a certain line, while north of it it should be excluded, and he saw an indisposition on the part of the country to stand upon that policy, and therefore he set about studying the subject upon original principles, and upon original principles he got up the Nebraska bill! I am fighting it upon these 'original principles' —fighting it in the Jeffersonian, Washingtonian and Madisonian fashion.

"Now, my friends, I wish you to attend for a little while to one or two other things in that Springfield speech. My main object was to show, so far as my humble ability was capable of showing to the people of this country, what I believe was the truth, that there was a tendency, if not a conspiracy among those who have engineered this slavery question for the last four or five years, to make slavery perpetual and universal in this nation.

"Having made that speech principally for that object, after arranging the evidences that I thought tended to prove my proposition, I concluded with this bit of comment: [Reads from Springfield speech].

"When my friend Judge Douglas came to Chicago, on the 9th of July, this speech having been delivered on the 16th of June, he made a harangue there, in which he took hold of the speech of mine, showing that he had carefully read it; and while he paid no attention to this matter at all, but complimented me as being a 'kind, amiable, and intelligent gentleman,' notwithstanding I had said this, he goes on and eliminates, or draws out, from my speech this tendency of mine to set the States at war with one another, to make all the institutions uniform, and set the niggers and white people to marrying together.

"Then, as the Judge had complimented me with these pleasant titles (I must confess to my weakness), I was a little 'taken,' for it came from a great man.

"I was not very much accustomed to flattery, and it came the sweeter to me.

"I was rather like the Hoosier with the gingerbread, when he said he loved it better than any other man and got less of it. As the Judge had so flattered me, I could not make up my mind that he meant to deal unfairly with me, so I went to work to show him that he misunderstood the whole scope of my speech, and that I really never intended to set the people at war with one another.

"As an illustration, the next time I met him, which was at Springfield, I used this expression, that I claimed no right under the Constitution, nor had I any inclination, to enter into the slave States and interfere with the institution of slavery.

"He says upon that: 'Lincoln will not enter into the slave States, but will go to the banks of the Ohio, on this side; and shoot over.' He runs on, step by step, in the horsechestnut style of argument, until in the Springfield speech he says, 'Unless he shall be successful in firing his batteries, until he shall have extinguished slavery in all the States, the Union shall be dissolved.' Now, I don't think that was exactly the way to treat a 'kind, amiable, intelligent gentleman.' I know if I had asked the Judge to show when and where it was I had said that, if I didn't succeed in firing into the slave States until slavery should be extinguished, the Union should be dissolved, he could not have shown it.

"I understand what he would do. He would say, 'I don't mean to quote from you, but this was the result of what you say.'

"But I have the right to ask, and I ask now, Did you not put it in such a form that an ordinary reader or listener would take it as an expression from me?

"In a speech at Springfield, on the night of the 17th, I thought I might as well attend to my own business a little, and I recalled his attention to the fact that he had acknowledged in my hearing twice that he had carefully read the speech, and still had put in no plea or answer. I took a default on him. I insisted that I had a right then to renew that charge of conspiracy. Ten days afterward I met the Judge at Clinton—that is to say, I was on the ground, but not in the discussion—I heard him make a speech.

"Then he comes in with his plea to this charge, for the first time, and his plea as put in, as well as I can recollect it, amounted to this: That he never had any talk with Judge Taney or the President of the United States with regard to the Dred Scott decision before it was made. I (Lincoln) ought to know that the man who makes a charge without knowing it to be true, falsifies as much as he who knowingly tells a falsehood; and lastly that he would pronounce the whole thing a falsehood; but he would make no personal application of the charge of falsehood, not because of any regard for the 'kind, amiable, intelligent gentleman,' but because of his own personal respect. I have understood since then—but [turning to Judge Douglas] will not hold the Judge to it if he is not willing—that he has broken through the 'self-respect,' and has got to saying the things out. The Judge nods to me that it is so.

"It is fortunate for me that I can keep as good-humored as I do, when the Judge acknowledged that he has been trying to make a question of veracity with me. I know the Judge is a great man, while I am only a small man, but I feel that I have got him. I demur to that plea. I waive all objections that it was not filed till after default was taken, and demur to it upon the merits. What if Judge Douglas never did talk with Chief Justice Taney and the President before the Dred Scott decision was made, does it follow that he could not have had as perfect an understanding without talking as with it?

"I am not disposed to stand upon my legal advantages. I am disposed to take his denial as being like an answer in chancery, that he neither had any knowledge, information nor belief in the existence of such a conspiracy.

"I am disposed to take his answer as being as broad as though he had put it in these words. And now, I ask, even if he had done so, have not I a right to prove it on him, and to offer the evidences of more than two witnesses, by whom to prove it; and if the evidence proves the existence of the conspiracy, does his broad answer denying all knowledge, information or belief, disturb the fact? It can only show that he was used by conspirators, and was not a leader of them.

"Now, in regard to reminding me of the moral rule that persons who tell what they do not know to be true falsify as much as those who knowingly tell falsehoods, I remember the rule, and it must be borne in mind that in what I have to read to you I do not say that I know such a conspiracy to exist. To that I reply, I believe it. If the Judge says that I do not believe it, then he says what he does not know, and falls within his own rule, that he who asserts a thing which he does not know to be true, falsifies as much as he who knowingly tells a falsehood. I want to call your attention to a little discussion on that branch of the case, and the evidence brought my mind to the conclusion which I expressed as my belief.

"If, in arraying that evidence, I had stated anything that was false or erroneous, it needed but that Judge Douglas should point it out, and I would have taken it back with all the kindness in the world.

"I do not deal in that way. If I have brought forward anything not a fact, if he will point it out, it will not even ruffle me to take it back.

"But if he will not point out anything erroneous in the evidence, is it not rather for him to show by a comparison of the evidence, that I have reasoned falsely, than to call the 'kind, amiable gentleman' a liar?

"If I have reasoned to a false conclusion, it is the vocation of an able debater to show by argument that I have wandered to an erroneous conclusion.

"I want to ask your attention to a portion of the Nebraska bill which Judge Douglas has quoted: 'It being the true intent and meaning of this act not to legislate slavery into any Territory or State, nor to exclude it therefrom; but to leave the people thereof perfectly free to form and regulate their domestic institutions in their own way, subject only to the Constitution of the United States.'

"Thereupon Judge Douglas and others began to argue in favor of 'Popular Sovereignty'—the right of the people to have slaves if they wanted them, and to exclude slavery if they did not want them.

" 'But,' said in substance a Senator from Ohio (Mr. Chase, I believe), 'we more than suspect that you do not mean to allow the people to exclude slavery, if they wish to, and if you do not mean it, accept an amendment which I propose, expressly authorizing the people to exclude slavery.'

"I believe I have the amendment before me, which was offered, and under which the people of the Territory, through their proper representatives, might, if they saw fit, prohibit the existence of slavery therein. And now I state it as a fact, to be taken back if there is any mistake about it, that Judge Douglas and those acting with him voted that amendment down. I now think that those men who voted it down had a real reason for doing so.

"They know what that reason was. It looks to us, since we have seen the Dred Scott decision pronounced, holding that 'under the Constitution' the people cannot exclude slavery—I say it looks to outsiders, poor, simple, 'amiable, intelligent gentlemen,' as though the niche was left as a place to put that Dred Scott decision in—a niche which would have been spoiled by adopting the amendment.

"And now, I say again, if this was not the reason, it will avail the Judge much more to calmly and good-humoredly point out to these people what that other reason was for voting the amendment down, than, swelling himself up, to vociferate that he may be provoked to call somebody a liar.

"Again, there is in that same quotation from the Nebraska bill this clause: 'It being the true intent and meaning of this bill not to legislate slavery into any Territory or State.'

"I have always been puzzled to know what business the word 'State' had in that connection. Judge Douglas knows. He put it there. He knows what he put it there for. We outsiders cannot say what he put it there for. The law that they were passing was not about States, and was not making provisions for States. What was it placed there for?

"After seeing the Dred Scott decision, which holds that the people cannot exclude slavery from a Territory, if another Dred Scott shall come, holding that they cannot exclude it from a State, we shall discover that when the word was originally put there, it was in view of something that was to come in due time, we shall see that it was the other half of something. I now say again, if there is any different reason for putting it there, Judge Douglas, in a good-humored way, without calling anybody a liar, can tell what the reason was.

"Quoting from Douglas's speech, 'When I saw that article in the Union on the 17th of November, and this clause in the Constitution asserting the doctrine that a State has no right to exclude slavery within its limits, I saw that there was a fatal blow being struck at the sovereignty of the States of this Union.' I stop the quotation there, again requesting that it may all be read.

"I have read all of the portion that I desire to comment upon.

"What is this charge that the Judge thinks I must have a very corrupt heart to make?

"It was the purpose on the part of certain high functionaries to make it impossible for the people of one State to prohibit the people of any other State from entering it with their 'property,' so called, and making it a slave State.

"In other words, it was a charge implying a design to make the institution of slavery national.

"And now I ask your attention to what Judge Douglas has himself done here. I know he made that part of the speech as a reason why he had refused to vote for a certain man for public printer, but when we get at it, the charge itself is the very one I made against him, that he thinks I am so corrupt for uttering.

"Now, whom does he make that charge against? Does he make it against that newspaper editor merely? No; he says it is identical in spirit with the Lecompston Constitution, and so the framers of that Constitution are brought in with the editor of the newspaper in that 'fatal blow being struck.'

"He did not call it a 'conspiracy.' In his language it is a 'fatal blow being struck.'

"And, if the words carry the meaning better when changed from a 'conspiracy' into a 'fatal blow being struck,' I will change my expression and change it to a 'fatal blow being struck.'

"We see the charge made not merely against the editor of the Union, but all the framers of the Lecompston Constitution, and not only so, but the article was an authoritative article. By whose authority?

"Is there any question but he means it was by the authority of the President and his Cabinet—the administration?

"Is there any sort of question but he means to make that charge? Then there are the editors of the Union, the framers of the Lecompston Constitution, the President of the United States and his Cabinet, and all the supporters of the Lecompston Constitution, in Congress and out of Congress, who are all involved in this 'fatal blow being struck.'

"I commend to Judge Douglas's consideration the question of how corrupt a man's heart must be to make such a charge!

"Now, my friends, I have but one branch of the subject, in the little time I have left, to which to call your attention, and as I shall come to a close at the end of that branch, it is probable that I shall not occupy all the time allotted to me. Although on these questions I would like to talk twice as long as I have, I could not enter upon another head and discuss it properly without running over my time.

"I ask the attention of the people here assembled and elsewhere, to the course that Judge Douglas is pursuing every day as bearing upon this question of making slavery national. Not going back to the records, but taking the speeches he makes, the speeches he made yesterday and the day before, and makes constantly all over the country—I ask your attention to them. In the first place, what is necessary to make the institution national? Not war. There is no danger that the people of Kentucky will shoulder their muskets, and, with a young nigger stuck on every bayonet, march to Illinois and force them upon us.

"There is no danger of our going over there and making war upon them. Then what is necessary for the nationalization of slavery?

"It is simply the next Dred Scott decision. It is merely for the Supreme Court to decide that no State under the

Constitution can exclude it, just as they have already decided that under the Constitution neither Congress nor the Territorial Legislature can do it. When that is decided and acquiesced in, the whole thing is done. This being true, and this being the way, as I think, that slavery is to be made national, let us consider what Judge Douglas is doing every day to that end.

"In the first place, let us see what influence he is exerting on public sentiment. In this and like communities, public sentiment is everything. With public sentiment, nothing can fail, without it, nothing can succeed. Consequently, he who molds public sentiment goes deeper than he who enacts statutes or pronounces decisions. He makes statutes and decisions possible or impossible to be executed. This must be borne in mind, as also the additional fact that Judge Douglas is a man of vast influence, so great that it is enough for many men to profess to believe anything when they once find out that Judge Douglas professes to believe it. Consider also the attitude he occupies at the head of a large party—a party which he claims has a majority of all the votes in the country. This man sticks to a decision, which forbids the people of a territory from excluding slavery, and he does so not because he says it is right in itself—he does not give any opinion on that—but because it has been decided by the court, and being decided by the court, he is, and you are, bound to take it in your political action as law—not that he judges at all of its merits, but because a decision of the court is to him a 'Thus saith the Lord.'

"He places it on that ground alone, and you will bear in mind that, thus committing himself unreservedly to this decision, he commits himself to the next one just as firmly as to this. He did not commit himself on account of the merit or demerit of the decision, but it is a 'Thus saith the Lord.' The next decision, as much as this, will be a 'Thus saith the Lord.'

"There is nothing that can divert or turn him away from this decision. It is nothing that I point out to him that his great prototype, General Jackson, did not so believe in the binding force of decisions. It is nothing that Jefferson did not so believe. I have said that I have often heard him approve of Jackson's course in disregarding the decision of the Supreme Court pronouncing a National Bank constitutional.

"He says I did not hear him say so. He denies the accuracy of my recollections. I say he ought to know better than I, but I will make no question about this thing, though it still seems to me that I heard him say it twenty times.

"I will tell him, though, that he now claims to stand on the Cincinnati platform, which affirms that Congress cannot charter a National Bank in the teeth of that old-standing decision that Congress can charter a bank. And I remind him of another piece of history on the question of respect for judicial decisions, and it is a piece of Illinois history, belonging to a time when the large party to which Judge Douglas belonged were displeased with a decision of the Supreme Court of Illinois, because they had decided that a Governor could not remove a Secretary of State. You will find the whole story in Ford's History of Illinois, and I know that Judge Douglas will not deny that he was then in favor of overruling that decision by the mode of adding five new Judges, so as to vote down the four old ones. Not only so, but it ended in the

Judge sitting down on that very bench as one of the five new Judges to break down the four old ones.

"It was in this way precisely that he got his title of Judge. Now, when the Judge tells me that men appointed conditionally to sit as members of a court will have to be catechised beforehand upon some subject, I say, 'You know, Judge; you have tried it.'

"When he says a court of this kind will lose the confidence of all men, will be prostituted and disgraced by such a proceeding, I say, 'You know best, Judge; you have been through the mill.' But I cannot shake Judge Douglas's teeth loose from the Dred Scott Decision.

"Like some obstinate animal (I mean no disrespect) that will hang on when he has once got his teeth fixed, you may cut off a leg, or you may tear away an arm, still he will not relax his hold. And so I may point out to the Judge, and say that he is bespattered all over, from the beginning of his political life to the present time, with attacks upon judicial decisions—I may cut off limb after limb of his public record, and strive to wrench him from a single dictum of the court—yet I cannot divert him from it. He hangs, to the last, to the Dred Scott decision. These things show there is a purpose strong as death and eternity, for which he adheres to this decision, and for which he will adhere to all other decisions of the same court."

A Hibernian—"Give us something beside Dred Scott."

Mr. Lincoln—"Yes; no doubt you want to hear something that don't hurt. Now, having spoken of the Dred Scott decision, one more word and I am done.

"Henry Clay, my beau-ideal of a statesman, the man for whom I fought all my humble life—Henry Clay once said of a class of men who would repress all tendencies to liberty and ultimate emancipation, that they must, if they would do this, go back to the era of our Independence, and muzzle the cannon which thunders its annual joyous return; they must blow out the moral lights around us; they must penetrate the human soul, and eradicate thence the love of liberty; and then, and not until then, could they perpetuate slavery in this country! To my thinking, Judge Douglas is, by his example and vast influence, doing that very thing in this vast community, when he says that the negro has nothing in the Declaration of Independence.

"Henry Clay plainly understood to the contrary. Judge Douglas is going back to the era of our Revolution, and, to the extent of his ability, muzzling the cannon which thunders its annual joyous return. When he invites any people, willing to have slavery, to establish it, he is blowing out the moral lights around us. When he says he 'cares not whether slavery is voted down or voted up'—that it is a sacred right of self-government—he is, in my judgment, penetrating the human soul and eradicating the light of reason and the love of liberty in this American people. And now I will only say that when, by all these means and appliances, Judge Douglas shall succeed in bringing public sentiment to an exact accordance with his own views—when these vast assemblages shall echo back all these sentiments—when they shall come to repeat his views and to avow his principles, and to say all that he says on these mighty questions—then it needs only the formality of the second Dred Scott decision, which he indorses in advance, to make slavery alike lawful in all the States—old as well as new, North as well as South.

"My friends, that ends the chapter. The Judge can take his half hour."

MR. DOUGLAS'S REPLY

(August 21, 1858)

"Fellow Citizens: I will now occupy the half-hour allotted to me in replying to Mr. Lincoln. The first point to which I will call your attention is, to what I said about the organization of the Republican party in 1854, and the platform that was formed on the 5th of October of that year, and I will then put the same question to Mr. Lincoln whether or not he approves of each article in that platform, and ask for a specific answer. I did not charge him with being a member of the Committee which reported that platform.

"I charged that that platform was the platform of the Republican party adopted by them.

"The fact that it was the platform of the Republican party is not denied, but Mr. Lincoln now says, that although his name was on the Committee which reported it, he does not think he was there, but thinks he was in Tazewell, holding court.

"Now I want to remind Mr. Lincoln, that he was at Springfield when that Convention was held and those resolutions adopted.

"The point I am going to remind Mr. Lincoln of is this: That after I had made my speech in 1854, during the fair, he gave me notice that he was going to reply to me the next day. I was sick at the time, but I stayed over in Springfield to hear his reply and to reply to him.

"On that day this very Convention, the resolutions

adopted, which I have read, was to meet in the Senate Chamber. He spoke in the hall of the House; and when he got through his speech—my recollection is distinct, and I shall never forget it—Mr. Codding walked in as I took the stand to reply, and gave notice that the Republican State Convention would meet instantly in the Senate Chamber, and called upon the Republicans to retire there and go into this very Convention, instead of remaining and listening to me.

"In the first place, Mr. Lincoln was selected by the very men who made the Republican organization, on that day, to reply to me.

"He spoke for them and for that party, and he was the leader of the party; and on the very day he made his speech in reply to me, preaching upon this same doctrine of negro equality, under the Declaration of Independence, this Republican party met in Convention.

"Another evidence that he was acting in concert with them is to be found in the fact that that Convention waited an hour after its time of meeting to hear Lincoln's speech, and Codding, one of their leading men, marched in the moment Lincoln got through, and gave notice that they did not want to hear me, and would proceed with the business of the Convention.

"Still another fact. I have here a newspaper printed at Springfield, Mr. Lincoln's own town, in October, 1854, a few days after the publishing of these resolutions, charging Mr. Lincoln with entertaining these sentiments, and trying to prove that they were also the sentiments of Mr. Yates, then candidate for Congress.

"This has been published on Mr. Lincoln over and over again, and never before has he denied it. But, my friends, this denial of his that he did not act on the committee, is a miserable quibble to avoid the main issue, which is, that this Republican platform declares in favor of the unconditional repeal of the Fugitive Slave Law. Has Mr. Lincoln answered whether he indorsed that or not? I called his attention to it when I first addressed you, and asked him for an answer, and then I predicted that he would not answer. How does he answer? Why, that he was not on the Committee that wrote the resolutions.

"I then repeated the next proposition contained in the resolutions, which was to restrict slavery in those States in which it exists, and asked him whether he indorsed it. Does he answer yes or no? He says in reply, 'I was not on the Committee at the time; I was up in Tazewell.'

"The next question I put to him was, whether he was in favor of prohibiting the admission of any more slave States into the Union.

"I put the question to him distinctly, whether, if the people of the Territory, when they had sufficient population to make a State, should form their Constitution recognizing slavery, he would vote for or against its admission. He is a candidate for the United States Senate, and it is possible, if he should be elected, that he would have to vote to admit a State into the Union, with slavery or without it, as its own people might choose. He did not answer that question. He dodges that question also, under the cover that he was not on the Committee at the time, that he was not present when the platform was made.

"I want to know, if he should happen to be in the Senate when a State applied for admission, with a Constitution acceptable to her own people, he would vote to admit that State, if slavery was one of its institutions. He avoids the answer. It is true, he gives the Abolitionists to understand by a hint that he would not vote to admit such a State. And why? He goes on to say that the man who would talk about giving each State the right to have slavery, or not, as it pleased, was akin to the man who would muzzle the guns which thundered forth the annual joyous return of the day of our independence.

"He says that that kind of talk is casting a blight on the glory of the country. What is the meaning of that? That he is not in favor of each State to have the right of doing as it pleases on the slavery question. I will put the questions to him again and again, and I intend to force it out of him.

"Then again, this platform which was made at Springfield by his own party, when he was its acknowledged head, provides that 'Republicans will insist on the abolition of slavery in the District of Columbia,' and I asked Lincoln specifically whether he agreed with them in that. ["Did you get an answer?"] He is afraid to answer it. He knows that I will trot him down to Egypt. I intend to make him answer there, or I will show the people of Illinois that he does not intend to answer these questions.

"The Convention to which I have been alluding goes a little further, and pledges itself to exclude slavery from all the Territories over which the General Government has exclusive jurisdiction north of 36 degrees 30 minutes, as well as south.

"Now I want to know whether he approves that provision. I want him to answer, and when he does, I want to know his opinion on another point, which is, whether he will redeem the pledge of the platform and resist the acquirement of any more territory, unless slavery therein shall be forever prohibited. I want him to answer the last question. Each of the questions I have put to him are practical questions, questions based upon the fundamental principles of the Black Republican party, and I want to know whether he is the first, last, and only choice of a party with whom he does not agree in principle.

"He does not deny but that that principle was unanimously adopted by the Republican party; he does not deny that the whole Republican party is pledged to it; he does not deny that a man who is not faithful to it is faithless to the Republican party; and I now want to know whether that party is unanimously in favor of a man who does not adopt that creed and agree with them in their principles. I want to know whether the man who does not agree with them, and who is afraid to avow his differences, and who dodges the issue, is the first, last, and only choice of the Republican party."

A voice—"How about the conspiracy?"

Mr. Douglas—"Never mind, I will come to that soon enough. But the plot from which I have read to you not only lays down these principles, but it adds:

" 'Resolved, That in furtherance of these principles we will use such Constitutional and lawful means as shall seem best adapted to their accomplishment, and that we will support no man for office, under the general or State Government, who is not positively and fully committed to the support of these principles, and whose personal character and conduct is not a guaranty that he is reliable, and who shall not have abjured old party allegiance and ties.'

"The Black Republican party stands pledged that they would never support Lincoln until he has pledged himself to that platform, but he cannot devise his answer; he has not made up his mind whether he will or not.

"He talked about everything else he could think of to occupy his hour and a half, and when he could not think of anything more to say, without an excuse for refusing to answer these questions, he sat down long before his time was out. In relation to Mr. Lincoln's charge of conspiracy against me, I have a word to say.

"In his speech to-day he quotes a playful part of his speech at Springfield, about Stephen and James, and Franklin and Roger, and says that I did not take exception to it. I did not answer it, and he repeats it again. I did not take exception to this figure of his.

"He has a right to be as playful as he pleases in throwing his arguments together, and I will not object; but I did take exception to his second Springfield speech, in which he stated that he intended his first speech as a charge of corruption or conspiracy against the Supreme Court of the United States, President Buchanan, and myself. That gave the offensive character to the charge. He then said that when he made it he did not know whether it was true or not, but inasmuch as Judge Douglas had not denied it, although he had replied to the other parts of his speech three times, he repeated it as a charge of conspiracy against me, thus charging me with moral turpitude. When he put it in that form, I did say, that inasmuch as he repeated the charge simply because I had not denied it, I would deprive him of the opportunity of ever repeating it again, by declaring that it was in all its bearings an infamous lie. He says he will repeat it until I answer his folly and nonsense about Stephen and Roger and Bob and James. He studied that out—prepared that one sentence with the greatest care, committed it to memory, and put it in his first Springfield speech, and now he carries that speech around and reads that sentence to show how pretty it is.

"His vanity is wounded because I will not go into that

beautiful figure of his about the building of a house. All I have to say is, that I am not green enough to let him make a charge which he acknowledges he does not know to be true, and then take up my time in answering it, when I know it to be false and nobody else knows it to be true. I have not brought a charge of moral turpitude against him. When he, or any other man, brings one against me, instead of disproving it, I will say that it is a lie, and let him prove it if he can. I have lived twenty-five years in Illinois. I have served you with all the fidelity and ability which I possess, and Mr. Lincoln is at liberty to attack my public action, my votes, and my conduct; but when he dares to attack my moral integrity, by a charge of conspiracy between myself, Chief-Justice Taney, and the Supreme Court, and two Presidents of the United States, I will repel it.

"Mr. Lincoln has not character enough for integrity and truth, merely on his ipse dixit, to arraign President Buchanan, President Pierce, and nine Judges of the Supreme Court, not one of whom would be complimented by being put on an equality with him.

"There is an unpardonable presumption in a man putting himself up before thousands of people, and pretending that his ipse dixit, without proof, without fact, and without truth, is enough to bring down and destroy the purest and best of living men.

"Fellow-citizens, my time is fast expiring; I must pass on. Mr. Lincoln wants to know why I voted against Mr. Chase's amendment to the Nebraska bill. I will tell him. In the first place, the bill already conferred all the power which Congress had, by giving the people the whole power over the subject. Chase offered a proviso that they might abolish slavery, which, by implication, would convey the idea that they could prohibit slavery by not introducing that institution.

"General Cass asked him to modify his amendment, so as to provide that the people might either prohibit or introduce slavery, and thus make it fair and equal.

"Chase refused to so modify his proviso, and then General Cass and all the rest of us voted it down. Those facts appear on the journals and debates of Congress, where Mr. Lincoln found the charge, and if he had told the whole truth, there would have been no necessity for me to occupy your time in explaining the matter.

"Mr. Lincoln wants to know why the word 'State' as well as 'Territory' was put in the Nebraska bill.

"I will tell him. It was put there to meet just such false arguments as he has been adducing.

"That, first, not only the people of the Territories should do as they pleased, but that when they came to be admitted as States, they should come into the Union with or without slavery, as the people determined. I meant to knock in the head the abolition doctrine of Mr. Lincoln's that there shall be no more slave States, even if the people want them. And it does not do for him to say, or for any other Black Republican to say, that there is nobody in favor of the doctrine of no more slave States, and that nobody wants to interfere with the right of the people to do as they please.

"What was the origin of the Missouri difficulty and the Missouri Compromise? The people of Missouri formed a Constitution as a slave State, and asked admission into the Union, but the Free Soil party of the North, being in a majority, refused to admit her because she had slavery as one of her institutions.

"Hence this first slavery agitation arose upon a State

and not upon a Territory, and yet Mr. Lincoln does not know why the word State was placed in the Kansas-Nebraska bill. The whole abolition agitation arose on that doctrine of prohibiting a State from coming in with slavery or not, as it pleased, and that same doctrine is here in this Republican platform of 1854; it has never been repealed; and every Black Republican stands pledged by that platform never to vote for any man who is not in favor of it. Yet Mr. Lincoln does not know that there is a man in the world who is in favor of preventing a State from coming in as it pleases, notwithstanding the Springfield platform says that they, the Republican party, will not allow a State to come in under such circumstances. He is an ignorant man.

"Now you see that upon these very points I am as far from bringing Mr. Lincoln up to the line as I ever was before. He does not want to avow his principles, I do want to avow mine, as clear as sunshine in midday. Democracy is founded upon the eternal principle of right. The plainer these principles are avowed before the people, the stronger will be the support which they will receive. I only wish I had the power to make them so clear that they would shine in the heavens for every man, woman, and child to read.

"The first of those principles that I would proclaim would be in opposition to Mr. Lincoln's doctrine of uniformity between the different States, and I would declare instead the sovereign right of each State to decide the slavery question as well as all other domestic questions for themselves, without interference from any other State or power whatsoever.

"When that principle is recognized you will have peace and harmony and fraternal feeling between all the States of this Union; until you do recognize that doctrine there will be sectional warfare agitating and distracting the country. What does Mr. Lincoln propose? He says that the Union cannot exist divided into free and slave States. If it cannot endure thus divided, then he must strive to make them all free or all slave, which will inevitably bring about the dissolution of the Union.

"Gentlemen, I am told that my time is out, and I am obliged to stop."

LINCOLN'S GREAT COOPER INSTITUTE SPEECH

Delivered at Cooper Institute, New York City, February 27, 1860. This speech, more than any other one, is supposed to have secured Lincoln the nomination for the Presidency.

"Mr. President and Fellow-Citizens of New York: The facts with which I shall deal this evening are mainly old and familiar; nor is there anything new in the general use I shall make of them. If there shall be any novelty, it will be in the mode of presenting the facts, and the references and observations following that presentation.

OUR FATHERS AND THE CONSTITUTION

"In his speech last autumn at Columbus, Ohio, as reported in the New York Times, Senator Douglas said:

" 'Our fathers, when they framed the Government under which we live, understood this question just as well and even better than we do now.'

"I fully endorse this, and I adopt it as a text for this discourse. I so adopt it because it furnishes a precise and agreed starting point for a discussion between Republicans and that wing of Democracy headed by Senator Douglas. It simply leaves the inquiry: 'What was the understanding those fathers had of the question mentioned? What is the frame of government under which we live?'

"The answer must be: 'The Constitution of the United States.'

"That Constitution consists of the original, framed in 1787 (and under which the present Government first went into operation), and twelve subsequently framed amendments, the first ten of which were framed in 1789.

"Who were our fathers who framed the Constitution? I suppose the 'thirty-nine' who signed the original instrument may be fairly called our fathers who framed that part of our present Government. It is almost exactly true to say they framed it, and it is altogether true to say they fairly represented the opinion and sentiment of the whole nation at that time. Their names, being familiar to nearly all, and accessible to quite all, need not be repeated.

"I take these 'thirty-nine,' for the present, as being 'our fathers who framed the Government under which we live.'

"What is the question which, according to the text, those fathers understood just as well and even better than we do now?

THE GREAT ISSUE

"It is this: Does the proper division of local from Federal authority, or anything in the Constitution, forbid our Federal Government to control us as to slavery in our Federal Territories?

"Upon this Douglas holds the affirmative, and Republicans the negative. This affirmative and denial form an issue; and this issue—this question—is precisely what the text declares our fathers understood better than we.

"In 1784—three years before the Constitution—the United States then owning the Northwestern Territory, and no other—the Congress of the Confederation had before them the question of prohibiting slavery in that Territory; and four of the 'thirty-nine' who afterward framed the Constitution were in that Congress, and voted on that question.

"Of these, Roger Sherman, Thomas Mifflin, and Hugh Williamson voted for the prohibition—thus showing that, in their understanding, no line divided local from Federal authority, nor anything else properly forbade the Federal Government to control as to slavery in Federal territory.

"The other of the four—James McHenry—voted against the prohibition, showing that, for some cause, he thought it improper to vote for it.

ORDINANCE OF 1787

"In 1787, still before the Constitution, but while the Convention was in session framing it, and while the Northwest Territory was the only territory owned by the United States, the same question of prohibiting slavery in the territory again came before the Congress of the Confederation, and three more of the 'thirty-nine' who afterward signed the Constitution were in that Congress, and voted on that question.

"They were: William Blount, William Few, and Abraham Baldwin, and they all voted for the prohibition—thus showing that, in their understanding, no line divided local from Federal authority, nor anything else properly forbade the Federal Government to control as to slavery in Federal territory. This time the prohibition became a law, being a part of what is now known as the ordinance of '87.

"The question of Federal control of slavery in the Territories seems not to have been directly before the convention which framed the original Constitution; and hence it is not recorded that the 'thirty-nine,' or any of them, while engaged on that instrument, expressed any opinion on that precise question.

THE FIRST CONGRESS

"In 1789, by the first Congress which sat under the Constitution, an act was passed to enforce the ordinance of '87, including the prohibition of slavery in the Northwestern Territory. The bill for this act was reported by one of the 'thirty-nine,' Thomas Fitzsimmons, then a member of the House of Representatives from Pennsylvania.

"It went through all its stages without a word of opposition, and finally passed both branches without yeas or nays, which is equivalent to a unanimous passage. In this Congress there were sixteen of the 'thirty-nine' fathers who framed the original Constitution.

"They were: John Langdon, Nicholas Gilman, William S. Johnson, Roger Sherman, Robert Morris, George Clymer, William Few, Abraham Baldwin, Rufus King, William Patterson, Richard Bassett, George Read, Pierce Butler, Daniel Carroll, James Madison, Thomas Fitzsimmons.

"This shows that in their understanding no line dividing local from Federal authority, nor anything in the Constitution, properly forbade Congress to prohibit slavery in the Federal territory, else both their fidelity to correct principle and their oath to support the Constitution would have constrained them to oppose the prohibition.

GEORGE WASHINGTON

"Again, George Washington, another of the 'thirty-nine,' was then President of the United States, and, as such, approved and signed the bill, thus completing its validity as a law, and thus showing that, in his understanding, no line dividing local from Federal authority, nor anything in the Constitution, forbade the Federal Government to control slavery in the Federal territory.

THE FIRST TERRITORIES

"No great while after the adoption of the original Constitution, North Carolina ceded to the Federal Government the country now constituting the State of Tennessee, and a few years later Georgia ceded that which now constitutes the States of Mississippi and Alabama. In both deeds of cession it was made a condition by the ceding States that the Federal Government should not prohibit slavery in the ceded country. Besides this, slavery was already in the ceded country. Under these circumstances, Congress, on taking charge of these countries, did not absolutely prohibit slavery within them. But they did interfere with it, take control of it, even there, to a certain extent.

"In 1798, Congress organized the Territory of Mississippi. In the act of organization they prohibited the bringing of slaves into the Territories from any place without the United States, by fine, and giving freedom to slaves so brought.

"This act passed both branches of Congress without yeas and nays. In that Congress were three of the 'thirty-nine' who framed the original Constitution. They were John Langdon, George Read, and Abraham Baldwin.

"They all, probably, voted for it. Certainly they would have placed their opposition to it upon the record if, in their understanding, any line dividing the local from Federal authority, or anything in the Constitution, properly forbade the Federal Government to control as to slavery in Federal territory.

THE LOUISIANA COUNTRY

"In 1803, the Federal Government purchased the Louisiana country. Our former territorial acquisitions came from certain of our own States; but this Louisiana country was acquired from a foreign nation. In 1804, Congress gave a territorial organization to that part of it which now constitutes the State of Louisiana. New Orleans, lying within that part, was an old and comparatively large city.

"There were other considerable towns and settlements, and slavery was extensively and thoroughly intermingled with the people. Congress did not, in the territorial act, prohibit slavery; but they did interfere with it—take control of it—in a more marked and extensive way than they did in the case of Mississippi. The substance of the provision therein made, in relation to slaves, was:

"First: That no slaves should be imported into the Territory from foreign parts.

"Second: That no slaves should be carried into it who

had been imported into the United States since the first day of May, 1798.

"Third: That no slave should be carried into it, except by the owner, and for his own use as a settler; the penalty in all the cases being a fine upon the violator of the law, and freedom to the slave.

"This act, also, was passed without yeas and nays. In the Congress which passed it there were two of the 'thirty-nine.' They were Abraham Baldwin and Jonathan Dayton. As stated in the case of Mississippi, it is probable they both voted for it; they would not have allowed it to pass without recording their opposition to it, if, in their understanding, it violated either the line properly dividing local from Federal authority, or any provision of the Constitution.

THE MISSOURI QUESTION

"In 1819-20 came, and passed, the Missouri question. Many votes were taken by yeas and nays, in both branches of Congress, upon the various phases of the general question.

"Two of the 'thirty-nine'—Rufus King and Charles Pinckney—were members of that Congress. Mr. King steadily voted for slavery prohibition and against all compromises. By this Mr. King showed that, in his understanding, no line dividing local from Federal authority, nor anything in the Constitution, was violated by Congress prohibiting slavery in Federal territory; while Mr. Pinckney, by his votes, showed that, in his understanding, there was some different reason for opposing such prohibition in the case.

"The cases I have already mentioned are the only acts

of the 'thirty-nine,' or any of them, upon the direct issue which I have been able to discover.

"To enumerate the persons who thus acted, as being four in 1784, three in 1787, seventeen in 1789, three in 1798, two in 1804, and two in 1819-20,—there would be thirty-one of them. But this would be counting John Langdon, Roger Sherman, William Few, Rufus King, and George Read, each twice, and Abraham Baldwin three times.

"The true number of those of the 'thirty-nine' whom I have shown to have acted upon the question, which, by the text, they understood better than we, is twenty-three, leaving sixteen not shown to have acted upon it in any way.

"Here, then, we have twenty-three of our 'thirty-nine' fathers who framed the Government under which we live, who have, upon their official responsibility and their corporal oaths, acted upon the very question which the text affirms they 'understood just as well, and even better than we do now'; and twenty-one of them—a clear majority of the whole 'thirty-nine'—so acting upon it as to make them guilty of a gross political impropriety and willful perjury, if, in their understanding, any proper division between local and Federal authority, or anything in the Constitution they had made themselves and sworn to support, forbade the Federal Government to control, as to slavery, in the Federal Territories. Thus the twenty-one acted; and, as actions speak louder than words, so actions under such responsibility speak still louder.

"Two of the twenty-three voted against Congressional prohibition of slavery in the Federal Territories, in the instances in which they acted upon the question. But for what reasons they so voted is not known. They may have done so because they thought a proper division of local from Federal authority, or some provision or principle of the Constitution, stood in the way; or they may, without any such question, have voted against the prohibition on what appeared to them to be sufficient grounds of inexpediency.

"No one who has sworn to support the Constitution can conscientiously vote for what he understands to be an unconstitutional measure, however expedient he may think it; but one may and ought to vote against a measure which he deems constitutional, if, at the same time, he deems it inexpedient.

"It, therefore, would be unsafe to set down even the two who voted against prohibition, as having done so, because, in their understanding, any proper division of local from Federal authority, or anything in the Constitution, forbade the Federal Government to control as to slavery in Federal Territory.

"The remaining sixteen of the 'thirty-nine,' so far as I have discovered, have left no record of their understanding upon the direct question of Federal control of slavery in the Federal Territories. But there is much reason to believe that their understanding upon that question would not have appeared different from that of their twenty-three compeers, had it been manifested at all.

"For the purpose of adhering rigidly to the text, I have purposely omitted whatever understanding may have been manifested by any person, however distinguished, other than the 'thirty-nine' fathers who framed the original Constitution; and, for the same reason, I have also omitted whatever understanding may have been manifested by any of the 'thirty-nine,' even on any other phase of the general question of slavery. If we should look into their acts and declarations on these other phases, as the foreign slave trade, and the morality and policy of slavery generally, it would appear to us that on the direct question of Federal control of slavery in Federal Territories, the sixteen, if they had acted at all, would probably have acted just as the twenty-three did. Among that sixteen were several of the most noted anti-slavery men of the times—as Dr. Franklin, Alexander Hamilton, and Gouverneur Morris—while there is not one now known to have been otherwise, unless it may have been John Rutledge, of South Carolina.

SUMMARY

"The sum of the whole is, that of our 'thirty-nine' fathers who framed the original Constitution, twenty-one—a clear majority of the whole—certainly understood that no proper division of local from Federal authority, nor any part of the Constitution, forbade the Federal Government to control slavery in the Federal Territories; while all the rest probably had the same understanding. Such, unquestionably, was the understanding of our fathers who framed the original Constitution; and the text affirms that they understood the question better than we.

AMENDMENT TO THE CONSTITUTION

"But, so far, I have been considering the understanding of the question manifested by the framers of the original Constitution. In and by the original instrument, a mode was provided for amending it; and, as I have already stated, the present frame of Government under which we live consists of that original and twelve amendatory articles framed and adopted since.

"Those who now insist that Federal control of slavery in Federal Territories violates the Constitution, point us to the provisions which they suppose it thus violates; and, as I understand, they all fix upon provisions in these amendatory articles, and not in the original instrument. The Supreme Court, in the Dred Scott case, plant themselves upon the fifth amendment, which provides that 'no person shall be deprived of property without due process of law'; while Senator Douglas and his peculiar adherents plant themselves upon the tenth amendment, providing that 'the powers granted by the Constitution are reserved to the States respectively, and to the people.'

"Now, it so happens that these amendments were framed by the first Congress which sat under the Constitution—the identical Congress which passed the act already mentioned, enforcing the prohibition of slavery in the Northwestern Territory. Not only was it the same Congress, but they were the identical, same individual men who, at the same session, and at the same time within the session, had under consideration, and in progress toward maturity, these constitutional amendments and this act prohibiting slavery in all the territory the nation then owned. The constitutional amendments were introduced before and passed after the act enforcing the ordinance of 1787, so that during the whole pendency of the act to enforce the ordinance, the constitutional amendments were also pending.

"That Congress, consisting of all the seventy-six members, including sixteen of the framers of the original Constitution, as before stated, were pre-eminently our fathers who framed that part of the Government under which we live, which is now claimed as forbidding the Federal Government to control slavery in the Federal Territories.

"Is it not a little presumptuous in any one at this day to affirm that the two things which that Congress deliberately framed, and carried to maturity at the same time, are absolutely inconsistent with each other? And does not such affirmation become impudently absurd with the other affirmation from the same mouth, that those who did the two things alleged to be inconsistent, understood whether they really were inconsistent better than we—better than he who affirms that they are inconsistent?

"It is surely safe to assume that the 'thirty-nine' framers of the original Constitution, and the seventy-six members of the Congress which framed the amendments thereto, taken together, do certainly include those who may be fairly called our fathers who framed the Government under which we live. And so assuming, I defy any man to show that any one of them ever in his whole life declared that, in his understanding, any proper division of local from Federal authority, or any part of the Constitution, forbade the Federal Government to control slavery in the Federal territories.

I GO A STEP FARTHER

"I go a step farther. I defy any one to show that any living man in the whole world ever did, prior to the beginning of the present century (and I might almost say prior to the beginning of the last half of the present century), declare that, in his understanding, any proper division of local from Federal authority, or any part of the Constitution, forbade the Federal Government to control as to slavery in the Federal Territories.

"To those who now so declare, I give, not only 'our fathers who framed the Government under which we live,' but with them all other living men within the century in which it was framed, among whom to search, and they shall not be able to find the evidence of a single man agreeing with them.

LET THERE BE NO MISUNDERSTANDING

"Now, and here, let me guard a little against being misunderstood. I do not mean to say we are bound to follow implicitly in whatever our fathers did. To do so would be to discard all the lights of current experiences —to reject all progress—all improvement. What I do say is, that if we would supplant the opinions and policy of our fathers in any case, we should do so upon evidence so conclusive, and argument so clear, that even their great authority, fairly considered and weighed, cannot stand, and most surely not in a case whereof we ourselves declare they understood the question better than we.

"If any man, at this day, sincerely believes that a proper division of local from Federal authority, or any part of the Constitution, forbids the Federal Government to control as to slavery in the Federal Territories, he is right to say so, and to enforce his position by all truthful evidence and fair argument which he can.

"But he has no right to mislead others, who have less access to history and less leisure to study it, into the false belief that 'our fathers who framed the Government under which we live' were of the same opinion—thus substituting falsehood and deception for truthful evidence and fair argument.

"If any man at this day sincerely believes 'our fathers

who framed the Government under which we live' used and applied principles, in other cases, which ought to have led them to understand that a proper division of local from Federal authority, or some part of the Constitution, forbids the Federal Government to control slavery in the Federal Territories, he is right to do so.

"But he should, at the same time, brave the responsibility of declaring that, in his opinion, he understands their principles better than they did themselves; and especially should he not shirk that responsibility by asserting that they 'understood the question just as well, and even better, than we do now.'

"But enough. Let all who believe that 'our fathers who framed the Government under which we live, understood this question just as well, and even better than we do now,' speak as they spoke, and act as they acted upon it. This is all Republicans ask—all Republicans desire—in relation to slavery. As those fathers marked it, so let it again be marked, as an evil not to be extended, but to be tolerated and protected only because of and so far as, its actual presence among us makes that toleration and protection a necessity. Let all the guarantees those fathers gave it, be, not grudgingly, but fully and fairly, maintained. For this Republicans contend, and with this, so far as I know or believe, they will be content.

A FEW WORDS FROM MR. LINCOLN TO THE SOUTHERN PEOPLE

"And now, if they would listen—as I suppose they will not—I would address a few words to the Southern people.

"I would say to them: You consider yourselves a reasonable and just people, and I consider that in the general qualities of reason and justice you are not inferior to any other people. Still, when you speak of us Republicans you do so only to denounce us as reptiles, or, at the best, as no better than outlaws. You will grant a hearing to pirates or murderers, but nothing like it to 'Black Republicans.' In all your contentions with one another, each of you deems an unconditional condemnation of 'Black Republicanism' as the first thing to be attended to. Indeed, such condemnation of us seems to be an indispensable prerequisite—license, so to speak—among you, to be admitted or permitted to speak at all.

"Now, can you, or not, be prevailed upon to pause and consider whether this is quite just to us, or even to yourselves?

"BRING FORWARD YOUR CHARGES"

"Bring forward your charges and specifications, and then be patient long enough to hear us deny or justify.

"You say we are sectional. We deny it. That makes an issue; and the burden of the proof is upon you. You produce your proof; and what is it? Why, that our party has no existence in your section—gets no votes in your section. The fact is substantially true; but does it prove the issue? If it does, then, in case we should, without change of principle, begin to get votes in your section, we should thereby cease to be sectional.

"You cannot escape this conclusion; and yet, are you willing to abide by it? If you are, you will probably soon find that we have ceased to be sectional, for we shall get votes in your section this very year. You will then begin to discover, as the truth plainly is, that your proof does not touch the issue.

"The fact that we get no votes in your section, is a fact of your own making, and not of ours; but this brings you to where you ought to have started—to a discussion of the right or wrong of our principle. If our principle, put in practice, would wrong your section for the benefit of ours, or for any other object, then our principle, and we with it, are sectional, and are justly exposed and denounced as such. Meet us, then, on the question of whether our principle, put in practice, would wrong your section; and so meet it as if it were possible that something may be said on our side.

"Do you accept the challenge? No? Then you really believe the principle which 'our fathers who framed the Government under which we live,' thought so clearly right as to adopt it and indorse it again and again, upon their official oaths, is, in fact, so clearly wrong as to demand your condemnation without a moment's consideration.

COULD WASHINGTON SPEAK, WHAT WOULD HE SAY?

"Some of you delight to flaunt in our faces the warning against sectional parties given by Washington in his Farewell Address. Less than eight years before Washington gave that warning, he had, as President of the United States, approved and signed an act of Congress enforcing the prohibition of slavery in the Northwestern Territory, which act embodied the policy of the Government upon that subject, up to and at, the very moment he penned that warning; and about one year after he penned it, he wrote Lafayette that he considered that prohibition a wise measure, expressing, in the same connection, his hope that we should at some time have a Confederacy of free States.

"Bearing this in mind, and seeing that sectionalism has since arisen on this same subject, is that warning a weapon in your hands against us, or in our hands against you? Could Washington himself speak, would he cast that blame of sectionalism upon us, who sustain his policy, or upon you, who repudiate it? We respect that warning of Washington, and we commend it to you, together with his example pointing to the right application of it.

WHAT IS CONSERVATISM?

"But you say you are conservative—eminently conservative—while we are revolutionary, destructive, or something of the sort. What is conservatism? Is it not adherence to the old and tried, against the new and untried? We stick to, contend for, the identical old policy, on the point of controversy, which was adopted by our fathers who framed the Government under which we live; while you, with one accord, reject, and scout, and spit upon that old policy, and insist upon substituting something new. True, you disagree among yourselves as to what that substitute shall be. You have considerable variety of new propositions and plans, but you are unanimous in rejecting and denouncing the old policy of the fathers.

"Some of you are for reviving the foreign slave trade; some for a Congressional slave code for the Territories; some for Congress forbidding the Territories to prohibit slavery within their limits; some for maintaining slavery in the Territories through the judiciary; some for the 'gur-reat pur-rinciple' that 'if one man should enslave another, no third man should object,' fantastically called 'Popular Sovereignty'; but never a man among you in favor of Federal prohibition of slavery in Federal Territories, according to the practice of our fathers who framed the Government under which we live.

"Not one of all your various plans can show a precedent or an advocate in the century within which our Government originated. Consider, then, whether your claim of conservatism for yourselves and your charge of destructiveness against us, are based on the most clear and stable foundations.

WE DENY IT

"Again, you say we have made the slavery question more prominent than it formerly was. We deny it. We admit that it is more prominent, but we deny that we made it so. It was not we, but you, who discarded the old policy of the fathers. We resisted, and still resist, your innovation, and thence comes the greater prominence of the question. Would you have that question reduced to its former proportions? Go back to that old policy. What has been will be again, under the same conditions. If you would have the peace of the old times, readopt the precepts and policy of the old times. You charge that we stir up insurrections among your slaves. We deny it; and what is your proof? Harper's Ferry! John Brown! John Brown was no Republican; and you have failed to implicate a single Republican in his Harper's Ferry enterprise.

"If any member of our party is guilty in that matter, you know it or you do not know it. If you do know it, you are inexcusable to not designate the man and prove the fact. If you do not know it, you are inexcusable to assert it, and especially to persist in the assertion after you have tried and failed to make the proof. You need not be told that persisting in a charge which one does not know to be true is simply malicious slander.

"WE DO NOT BELIEVE IT"

"Some of you admit that no Republican designedly aided or encouraged the Harper's Ferry affair, but still insist that our doctrines and declarations necessarily lead to such results. We do not believe it. We know we hold to no doctrines and make no declarations which were not held to and made by our fathers who framed the Government under which we live. You never dealt fairly by us in relation to this affair. When it occurred, some important State elections were near at hand, and you were in evident glee with the belief that by charging the blame upon us you could get an advantage of us in those elections. The elections came, and your expectations were not fulfilled. Every Republican man knew that, as to himself at least, your charge was a slander, and he was not much inclined by it to cast his vote in your favor. Republican doctrines and declarations are accompanied with a continual protest against any interference whatever with your slaves, or with you about your slaves.

"Surely this does not encourage them to revolt. True, we do, in common with our fathers who framed the Government under which we live, declare our belief that slavery is wrong; but the slaves do not hear us declare even this. For anything we say or do the slaves would scarcely know that there was a Republican party. I believe they would not, in fact, generally know it but for your misrepresentations of us in their hearing. In your political contests among yourselves, each faction charges the other with sympathy with Black Republicanism; and then, to give point to the charge, defines Black Republicanism to simply be insurrection, blood and thunder among the slaves.

INSURRECTION IMPOSSIBLE

"Slave insurrections are no more common now than they were before the Republican party was organized. What induced the Southampton insurrection, twenty-eight years ago, in which at least three times as many lives were lost as at Harper's Ferry? You can scarcely stretch your very elastic fancy to the conclusion that Southampton was got up by Black Republicanism. In the present state of things in the United States, I do not think a general or even a very extensive slave insurrection is possible. The indispensable concert of action cannot be attained. The slaves have no means of rapid communication; nor can incendiary free men, black or white, supply it. The explosive materials are everywhere in parcels; but there neither are, nor can be supplied, the indispensable connecting trains.

"Much is said by Southern people about the affection of slaves for their masters and mistresses; and a part of it, at least, is true. A plot for an uprising could scarcely be devised and communicated to twenty individuals before some one of them, to save the life of a favorite master or mistress, would divulge it. This is the rule; and a slave revolution in Hayti was not an exception to it, but a case occurring under peculiar circumstances. The gunpowder plot of British history, though not connected with slaves, was more in point. In that case only about twenty were admitted to the secret; and yet one of them, in his anxiety to save a friend, betrayed the plot to that friend, and, by consequence, averted the calamity.

"Occasional poisonings from the kitchen, and open or stealthy assassinations in the field, and local revolt extended to a score or so, will continue to occur as the natural results of slavery, but no general insurrection of slaves, as I think, can happen in this country for a long time. Whoever much fears, or much hopes, for such an event, will be alike disappointed.

"In the language of Mr. Jefferson, uttered many years ago, 'It is still in our power to direct the process of emancipation and deportation peaceably, and in such slow degrees, as that the evil will wear off insensibly; and their places be, pari passu, filled up by free white laborers. If, on the contrary, it is left to force itself on, human nature must shudder at the prospect held up.'

"Mr. Jefferson did not mean to say, nor do I, that the power of emancipation is in the Federal Government. He spoke of Virginia, and, as to the power of emancipation, I speak of the slave-holding States only.

"The Federal Government, however, as we insist, has the power of restraining the extension of the institution —the power to insure that a slave insurrection shall never occur on any American soil which is now free from slavery.

JOHN BROWN

"John Brown's effort was peculiar. It was not a slave insurrection. It was an attempt by white men to get up a revolt among slaves, in which the slaves refused to participate. In fact, it was so absurd that the slaves, with all their ignorance, saw plainly enough that it could not succeed. That affair, in its philosophy, corresponds with the many attempts related in history, at the assassination of kings and emperors. An enthusiast broods over the oppression of a people till he fancies himself commissioned by Heaven to liberate them. He ventures the attempt, which ends in little else than in his own execution.

"Orsini's attempt on Louis Napoleon, and John Brown's attempt at Harper's Ferry, were, in their philosophy, precisely the same. The eagerness to cast blame on old England in the one case, and on New England in the other, does not disprove the sameness of the two things.

"And how much would it avail you if you could, by the use of John Brown, Helper's Book, and the like, break up the Republican organization? Human action can be modified to some extent, but human nature cannot be changed. There is a judgment and a feeling against slavery in this nation, which cast at least a million and a half votes! You cannot destroy that judgment and feeling—that sentiment—by breaking up the political organization which rallies around it.

"You can scarcely scatter and disperse an army which has been formed into order in the face of your heaviest fire; but if you could, how much would you gain by forcing the sentiment which created it out of the peaceful channel of the ballot-box into some other channel? What would that other channel probably be? Would the number of John Browns be lessened or enlarged by the operation?

"RULE OR RUIN"

"But you will break up the Union, rather than submit to a denial of your Constitutional rights.

"That has a somewhat reckless sound; but it would be palliated, if not fully justified, were we proposing, by the mere force of numbers, to deprive you of some right, plainly written down in the Constitution. But we are proposing no such thing.

"When you make these declarations, you have a specific and well-understood allusion to an assumed Constitutional right of yours, to take slaves into the Federal Territories, and to hold them there as property. But no such right is specifically written in the Constitution. That instrument is literally silent about any such right. We, on the contrary, deny that such a right has any existence in the Constitution, even by implication.

"Your purpose, then, plainly stated, is, that you will destroy the Government unless you be allowed to construe and enforce the Constitution as you please, on all the points in dispute between you and us. You will rule or ruin in all events. This, plainly stated, is your language to us.

"NOT QUITE SO"

"Perhaps you will say the Supreme Court has decided the disputed constitutional question in your favor. Not quite so. But, waiving the lawyer's distinction between dictum and decision, the court has decided the question for you in a sort of way. The court has substantially said it is your Constitutional right to take slaves into the Federal Territories, and to hold them there as property.

"When I say the decision was made in a sort of way, I mean it was made in a divided court, by a bare majority of the judges, and they not quite agreeing with one another; that its avowed supporters disagree with one another about its meaning; and that it was mainly based upon a mistaken statement of fact—the statement in the opinion that 'the right of property in a slave is distinctly and expressly affirmed in the Constitution.'

"An inspection of the Constitution will show that the right of property in a slave is not distinctly and expressly affirmed in it. Bear in mind, the judges do not pledge their judicial opinion that such right is implicitly affirmed in the Constitution; but they pledge their veracity that it is distinctly and expressly affirmed there—'distinctly'—that is, not mingled with anything else—'expressly'—that is, in words meaning just that, without the aid of any inference, and susceptible of no other meaning.

"If they had only pledged their judicial opinion, that such right is affirmed in the instrument by implication, it would be open to others to show that, neither the word 'slave,' nor 'slavery,' is to be found in the Constitution, nor the word 'property' even, in any connection with language alluding to the things slave or slavery, and that wherever, in that instrument, the slave is alluded to, he is called 'a person,' and wherever his master's legal right in relation to him is alluded to, it is spoken of as 'service or labor due,' as a 'debt' payable in service or labor.

"Also, it would be open to show, by contemporaneous history, that this mode of alluding to slaves and slavery, instead of speaking of them, was employed on purpose to exclude from the Constitution the idea that there could be property in man.

"To show all this is easy and certain.

"When the obvious mistake of the judges shall be brought to their notice, is it not reasonable to expect that they will withdraw the mistaken statement, and reconsider the conclusion based upon it?

"And then it is to be remembered that 'our fathers who framed the Government under which we live'—the men who made the Constitution—decided this same Constitutional question in our favor, long ago—decided it without a division among themselves about the meaning of it after it was made, so far as any evidence is left, without basing it upon any mistaken statements of facts.

"Under all these circumstances, do you really feel yourself justified to break up this Government, unless such a court decision as yours is shall be at once submitted to as a conclusive and final rule of political action?

"But you will not abide the election of a Republican President! In that supposed event, you say, you will destroy the Union; and then, you say, the great crime of having destroyed it will be upon us?

"This is cool. A highwayman holds a pistol to my ear, and mutters through his teeth, 'Stand and deliver, or I shall kill you, and then you will be a murderer!'

"To be sure, what the robber demanded of me—my money—was my own, and I had a clear right to keep it; but it was no more my own than my vote is my own; and the threat of death to me, to extort my money, and the threat of destruction to the Union, to extort my vote, can scarcely be distinguished in principle.

A FEW WORDS TO THE REPUBLICANS

"A few words now to Republicans. It is exceedingly desirable that all parts of this great Confederacy shall be at peace, and in harmony, with one another. Let us Republicans do our part to have it so. Even though much provoked, let us do nothing through passion and ill-temper. Even though the Southern people will not so much as listen to us, let us calmly consider their demand, and yield to them, if, in our deliberate view of our duty, we possibly can. Judging by all they say and do, and by the subject and nature of their controversy with us, let us determine, if we can, what will satisfy them.

"Will they be satisfied if the Territories be unconditionally surrendered to them? We know they will not.

In all their present complaints against us, the Territories are scarcely mentioned. Invasions and insurrections are the rage now. Will it satisfy them if, in the future, we have nothing to do with invasions and insurrections? We know it will not. We so know because we know we never had anything to do with invasions and insurrections; and yet this total abstaining does not exempt us from the charge and the denunciation.

"The question recurs, what will satisfy them? Simply this: We must not only let them alone, but we must, somehow, convince them that we do let them alone. This we know by experience is no easy task. We have been so trying to convince them from the very beginning of our organization, but with no success. In all our platform and speeches, we have constantly protested our purpose to let them alone; but this had no tendency to convince them. Alike unavailing to convince them is the fact that they have never detected a man of us in any attempt to disturb them.

"These natural and apparently adequate means all failing, what will convince them? This, and this only: Cease to call slavery wrong, and join them in calling it right. And this must be done thoroughly—done in acts as well as words. Silence will not be tolerated—we must place ourselves avowedly with them. Douglas's new sedition law must be enacted, and enforced, suppressing all declarations that slavery is wrong, whether made in politics, in presses, in pulpits, or in private. We must arrest and return their fugitive slaves with greedy pleasure. We must pull down our Free State Constitutions. The whole atmosphere must be disinfected from all taint of opposition to slavery, before they will cease to believe that all their troubles proceed from us.

"I am quite aware they do not state their case precisely in this way. Most of them would probably say to us, 'Let us alone, do nothing to us, and say what you please about slavery.' But we do let them alone—have never disturbed them—so that, after all, it is what we say which dissatisfies them. They will continue to accuse us of doing until we cease saying.

"I am also aware they have not, as yet, in terms, demanded the overthrow of our Free State Constitutions. Yet those constitutions declare the wrong of slavery with more solemn emphasis than do all other sayings against it; and when all other sayings shall have been silenced, the overthrow of these constitutions will be demanded, and nothing be left to resist the demand. It is nothing to the contrary that they do not demand the whole of this just now. Demanding what they do, and for the reason they do, they can voluntarily stop nowhere short of this consummation. Holding, as they do, that slavery is morally and socially elevating, they cannot cease to demand a full national recognition of it, as a legal right and a social blessing.

"Nor can we justifiably withhold this on any ground, save our conviction that slavery is wrong. If slavery is right, all words, acts, laws, and Constitutions against it are themselves wrong, and should be silenced and swept away. If it is right, we cannot justly object to its nationality—its universality; if it is wrong, they cannot justly insist upon its extension—its enlargement. All they ask we could readily grant, if we thought slavery right; all we ask they could as readily grant, if they thought it wrong.

"Their thinking it right, and our thinking it wrong, is the precise fact upon which depends the whole controversy. Thinking it right, as they do, they are not to blame for desiring its full recognition, as being right; but thinking it wrong, as we do, can we yield to them? Can we cast our votes with their view and against our own? In view of our moral, social, and political responsibility, can we do this?

"Wrong as we may think slavery is, we can yet afford to let it alone where it is, because that much is due to the necessity arising from its actual presence in the nation; but can we, while our votes will prevent it, allow it to spread into the national Territories, and to overrun us here in these free States?

"If our sense of duty forbids this, then let us stand by our duty fearlessly and effectively. Let us be diverted by none of those sophistical contrivances wherewith we are so industriously plied and belabored—contrivances, such as groping for some middle ground between the right and the wrong, vain as the search for a man who should be neither a living man nor a dead man—such as a policy of "don't care" on a question about which all true men do care—such as Union appeals, beseeching true Union men to yield to disunionists, reversing the divine rule, and calling, not the sinners, but the righteous to repentance—such as invocations of Washington—imploring men to unsay what Washington said—and undo what Washington did.

"Neither let us be slandered from our duty by false accusations against us, nor frightened from it by menaces of destruction to the Government, nor of dungeons to ourselves.

"Let us have faith that Right makes Might; and in that faith let us to the end dare to do our duty as we understand it."

FIRST SPEECH AFTER HIS NOMINATION

(To the Committe, Springfield, Ill., May 19, 1860)

"Mr. Chairman and Gentlemen of the Committee: I tender to you, and through you, to the Republican National Convention, and all the people represented in it, my profoundest thanks for the high honor done me, which you now formally announce. Deeply and even painfully sensible of the great responsibility which I could wish had fallen upon some one of the far more eminent men and experienced statesmen whose distinguished names were before the Convention, I shall, by your leave, consider more fully the resolutions of the Convention denominated the platform, and, without unnecessary and unreasonable delay, respond to you, Mr. Chairman, in writing, not doubting that the platform will be found satisfactory and the nomination gratefully accepted. And now I will not longer defer the pleasure of taking you, and each of you, by the hand."

PRESIDENT LINCOLN'S ADIEU TO SPRINGFIELD

On Monday, February 11, 1861, at 8 a.m., President Lincoln left Springfield. After exchanging a parting salutation with his wife, he took his stand on the platform, removed his hat, and, asking silence, spoke as follows to the multitude that stood in respectful silence and with their heads uncovered:

"My Friends: No one, not in my position, can appreciate the sadness I feel at this parting. To this people I owe all that I am. Here I have lived more than a quarter of a century, here my children were born and here one of them lies buried.

"I know not how soon I shall see you again. A duty devolves upon me, which is, perhaps, greater than has devolved upon any other man since the days of Washington.

"He never could have succeeded except for the aid of Divine Providence, upon which he at all times relied. I feel that I cannot succeed without the same Divine aid which sustained him; and in the same Almighty Being I place my reliance for support, and I hope you, my friends, will all pray that I may receive that Divine assistance without which I cannot succeed, but with which, success is certain.

"Again, I bid you all an affectionate farewell." (Loud applause and cries of, "We will pray for you.")

Towards the conclusion of the remarks, himself and audience were moved to tears. His exhortation to pray elicited choked exclamations of, "We will do it, we will do it!" As he turned to enter the cars, three cheers were given, and a few seconds afterward the train moved slowly out of the sight of the silent gathering.

SPEECH DELIVERED AT CINCINNATI, FEBRUARY 12, 1861.

"I have spoken but once, before this, in Cincinnati. That was a year previous to the great Presidential election. On that occasion, in a playful manner, but with sincere words, I addressed much of what I said to the Kentuckians. I gave my opinion, that we, as Republicans, would ultimately beat them as Democrats, but that they could postpone that result longer by nominating Senator Douglas for the Presidency than they could in any other way. They did not in any true sense of the word nominate Mr. Douglas, and the result has come certainly as soon as ever I expected.

"I also told them how I expected they would be treated after they should have been beaten; and now I wish to call their attention to what I then said upon the subject. I then said: 'When we do as we say, beat you, you perhaps want to know what we will do with you. I will tell you, as for as I am authorized to speak for the opposition, what we mean to do with you. We mean to treat you, as near as we possibly can, as Washington, Jefferson, and Madison treated you. We mean to leave you alone, and in no way to interfere with your institutions; to abide by all and every compromise of the Constitution, and, in a word, coming back to the original proposition, to treat you so far as degenerate men, if we have degenerated, may according to the example of those noble fathers, Washington, Jefferson, and Madison.

" 'We mean to remember that you are as good as we; that there is no difference of circumstances. We mean to recognize and bear in mind always that you have as good hearts in your bosoms as other people, or as we claim to have, and treat you accordingly.' Fellow citizens of Kentucky—friends and brethren, may I call you in your new position?—I see no occasion and feel no inclination to retract a word of this. If it shall not be made good, be assured the fault shall not be mine."

LINCOLN'S SPEECH AT INDIANAPOLIS, FEBRUARY 12, 1861.

"Fellow Citizens of the State of Indiana: I am here to thank you very much for the magnificent welcome, and still more for the generous support given by your State to that political cause which I think is the true and just cause of the whole country and the whole world.

"Solomon says there is a time to keep silence, and when men wrangle by the month, with no certainty that they mean the same thing while using the same word, it perhaps were as well if they would keep silence.

"The words coercion and invasion are much used in these days and often with some temper and hot blood.

"Let us make sure, if we can, that we do not misunderstand the meaning of those who use them. Let us get the exact definition of the words, not from the dictionaries, but from the men themselves, who certainly deprecate the things they would represent by the use of the words. What, then, is coercion? What is invasion? Would the marching of an army into South Carolina, without the consent of her people and with hostile intent towards them, be invasion? I certainly think it would; and it would be coercion also if the South Carolinians were forced to submit. But if the United States should merely hold and retain its own forts and other property, and collect the duty on foreign importations, or even withhold the mails from places where they were habitually violated —would any or all these things be 'invasion' or 'coercion'?

"Do our professed lovers of the Union, but who spitefully resolve that they will resist coercion and invasion, understand that such things as these, on the part of the

United States, would be coercion or invasion of a State? If so, their ideas of means to preserve the object of their great affection would seem to be exceedingly thin and airy. If sick, the little pills of the homeopathist would be much too large for it to swallow. In their view, the Union, as a family relation, would seem to be no regular marriage, but rather a sort of free love arrangement to be maintained on passionate attraction.

"By the way, in what consists the special sacredness of a State? I speak not of the position assigned to the State in the Union by the Constitution, for that, by the bond, we all recognize.

"That position, however, a State cannot carry out of the Union with it.

"I speak of that assumed primary right of a State to rule all which is less than itself, and to ruin all that is larger than itself.

"If a State and a county, in a given case, should be equal in extent of territory, and equal in number of inhabitants, in what, as a matter of principle, is the State better than the county? Would an exchange of names be an exchange of rights upon principles? On what rightful principle, may a State, being not more than one-fiftieth part of the nation in soil and population, break up the nation, and then coerce a proportionally larger subdivision of itself, in the most arbitrary way? What mysterious right to play tyrant is conferred on a district of country with its people by merely calling it a State? Fellow-citizens, I am not asserting anything. I am merely asking questions for you to consider, and now allow me to bid you farewell."

LINCOLN'S SPEECH AT COLUMBUS, OHIO, ON THIRTEENTH OF FEBRUARY, 1861

He thus spoke to the Legislature and public:

"Mr. President, and Mr. Speaker, and Gentlemen of the General Assembly: It is true, as has been said by the President of the Senate, that a very great responsibility rests upon me in the position to which the votes of the American people have called me.

"I am deeply sensible of that weighty responsibility. I cannot but know what you all know, that without a name, perhaps without a reason why I should have a name, there has fallen upon me a task such as did not rest even upon the Father of his Country; and so feeling, I cannot but turn and look for that support without which it will be impossible for me to perform that great task. I turn, then, and look to the American people, and to that God who has never forsaken them. Allusions have been made to the interest felt in relation to the policy of the new Administration. In this I have received from some a degree of credit for having kept silence and from others deprecation. I still think I was right. In the varying and repeatedly shifting scenes of the present, and without a precedent which could enable me to judge by the past, it has seemed fitting, that, before speaking upon the difficulties of the country, I should have gained a view of the whole field, so as to be sure, after all—at liberty to modify and change the course of policy, as future events may make a change necessary. I have not maintained silence from any want of real anxiety. It is a good thing that there is no more than anxiety, for there is nothing going wrong. It is a consoling circumstance that when we look out there is nothing that really hurts anybody. We entertain different views upon political questions, but nobody is suffering in anything. This is a most consoling circumstance, and from it we may conclude that all we want is time, patience, and a reliance on that God who has never forsaken this people.

"Fellow-citizens, what I have said, I have said extemporaneously, and will now come to a close."

LINCOLN'S SPEECH IN WASHINGTON

Delivered Wednesday, February 27, 1861, at his hotel. On Wednesday, the 27th, the Mayor and Common Council of the city waited upon Mr. Lincoln and tendered him a welcome. He replied to them as follows:

"Mr. Mayor: I thank you, and through you the municipal authorities of this city who accompany you, for this welcome. And as it is the first time in my life since the present phase of politics has presented itself in this country, that I have said anything publicly within a region of country where the institution of slavery exists, I will take this occasion to say that I think very much of the ill feeling that has existed and still exists between the people in the sections from which I came and the people here, is dependent upon a misunderstanding of one another. I therefore avail myself of this opportunity to assure you, Mr. Mayor, and all the gentlemen present, that I have not now, and never have had, any other than as kindly feelings towards you as the people of my own section. I have not now, and never have had, any disposition to treat you in any respect otherwise than as my own neighbors. I have not now any purpose to withhold from you any of the benefits of the Constitution, under any circumstances, that I would not feel myself constrained to withhold from my own neighbors; and I hope, in a word, that when we shall become better acquainted —and I say it with great confidence—we shall like each other the more. I thank you for the kindness of this reception."

FIRST TALK AFTER HIS NOMINATION

The telegram was received in the Journal office at Springfield. Immediately everybody wanted to shake his hand; and so long as he was willing, they continued to congratulate him.

"Gentlemen [with a twinkle in his eye]: You had better come up and shake my hand while you can; honors elevate some men, you know. . . . Well, gentlemen, there is a little woman at our house who is probably more interested in this dispatch than I am; and if you will excuse me, I will take it up to her and let her read it."

LINCOLN'S FIRST INAUGURAL ADDRESS

Delivered March 4, 1861, at Washington:

"Fellow Citizens of the United States: In compliance with a custom as old as the Government itself, I appear before you to address you briefly, and to take, in your presence, the oath prescribed by the Constitution of the United States to be taken by the President before he enters on the execution of his office.

POSITION STATED

"I do not consider it necessary, at present, for me to discuss those matters of administration about which there is no special anxiety or excitement. Apprehension seems to exist among the people of the Southern States that, by the accession of a Republican administration, their property and their peace and personal security are to be endangered. There has never been any reasonable cause for such apprehension. Indeed, the most ample evidence to the contrary has all the while existed, and been open to their inspection. It is found in nearly all the published speeches of him who now addresses you. I do but quote from one of those speeches, when I declare that 'I have no purpose, directly or indirectly, to interfere with the institution of slavery in the States where it exists.' I believe I have no lawful right to do so. Those who nominated and elected me did so with the full knowledge that I had made this, and made many similar declarations, and had never recanted them. And, more than this, they placed in the platform, for my acceptance, and as a law to themselves and to me, the clear and emphatic resolution which I now read:

"'Resolved, That the maintenance inviolate of the right of the States, and especially the right of each State, to order and control its own domestic institutions according to its own judgment exclusively, is essential to that balance of power on which the perfection and endurance of our political fabric depend; and we denounce the lawless invasion by armed force of the soil of any State or Territory, no matter under what pretext, as among the gravest of crimes.'

"I now reiterate these sentiments; and in doing so I only press upon the public attention the most conclusive evidence of which the case is susceptible, that the property, peace, and security of no section are to be in any wise endangered by the now incoming administration.

"I add, too, that all the protection, which, consistently with the Constitution and the laws, can be given, will be given to all the States when lawfully demanded, for whatever cause, as cheerfully to one section as to another.

"There is much controversy about the delivering up of fugitives from service or labor. The clause I now read is as plainly written in the Constitution as any other of its provisions:

" 'No person held to service or labor in one State under the laws thereof, escaping into another, shall, in consequence of any law or regulation therein, be discharged from such service or labor, but shall be delivered up on claim of the party to whom such service or labor may be due.'

"It is scarcely questioned that this provision was intended by those who made it for the reclaiming of what we call fugitive slaves; and the intention of the lawgiver is the law.

"All the members of Congress swear their support to the whole Constitution—to this provision as well as any other.

"To the proposition, then, that slaves whose cases come within the terms of this clause, 'shall be delivered up,' their oaths are unanimous. Now, if they would make the effort in good temper, could they not, with nearly equal unanimity, frame and pass a law by means of which to keep good that unanimous oath?

"There is some difference of opinion whether this clause should be enforced by national or by State authority; but surely that difference is not a very material one.

"If the slave is to be surrendered, it can be of little consequence to him or to others by which authority it is done; and should any one, in any case, be content that this oath shall go unkept on a mere inconsequential controversy as to how it shall be kept?

"Again, in any law upon this subject, ought not all the safeguards of liberty known in civilized and humane jurisprudence to be introduced, so that a free man be not, in any case, surrendered as a slave? And might it not be well at the same time to provide by law for the enforcement of that clause in the Constitution which guarantees that 'the citizens of each State shall be entitled to all the privileges and immunities of citizens in the several States'?

NO MENTAL RESERVATION

"I take the official oath to-day with no mental reservations, and with no purpose to construe the Constitution or laws by any hypercritical rules; and while I do not choose now to specify particular acts of Congress as proper to be enforced, I do suggest that it will be much safer for all, both in official and private stations, to conform to and abide by all those acts which stand unrepealed, than to violate any of them, trusting to find impunity in having them held to be unconstitutional.

"It is seventy-two years since the first inauguration of a President under our national Constitution. During that period fifteen different and very distinguished citizens have in succession administered the executive branch of the Government. They have conducted it through many perils, and generally with great success. Yet, with all this scope for precedent, I now enter upon the same task for the brief Constitutional term of four years, under great and peculiar difficulties.

I HOLD THE UNION OF THESE STATES IS PERPETUAL

"A disruption of the Federal Union, heretofore only menaced, is now formidably attempted. I hold that in the contemplation of universal law and of the Constitution, the Union of these States is perpetual. Perpetuity is implied, if not expressed, in the fundamental law of all national governments. It is safe to assert that no government proper ever had a provision in its organic law for its own termination. Continue to execute all the express provisions of our national Constitution, and the Union will endure forever, it being impossible to destroy except by some action not provided for in the instrument itself.

"Again, if the United States be not a government proper, but an association of States in the nature of a contract merely, can it, as a contract, be peaceably unmade by less than all the parties who made it? One party to a contract may violate it—break it, so to speak; but does it not require all to lawfully rescind it? Descending from these general principles, we find the proposition that in legal contemplation the Union is perpetual, confirmed by the history of the Union itself.

"The Union is much older than the Constitution. It was formed, in fact, by the Articles of Association in 1774. It was matured and continued in the Declaration of Independence in 1776. It was further matured, and the faith of all the then thirteen States expressly plighted and engaged that it should be perpetual, by the Articles of the Confederation in 1778; and, finally, in 1787, one of the declared objects for ordaining and establishing the Constitution was 'to form a more perfect union.' But if destruction of the Union by one, or by a part only of the States, be lawfully possible, the union is less perfect than before, the Constitution having lost the vital element of perpetuity.

"It follows from these views, that no State, upon its own mere motion, can lawfully get out of the Union; that resolves and ordinances to that effect are legally void, and the acts of violence within any State or States, against the authority of the United States, are insurrectionary or revolutionary, according to circumstances.

"I, therefore, consider that, in view of the Constitution and the laws, the Union is unbroken, and to the extent of my ability, I shall take care, as the Constitution itself expressly enjoins upon me, that the laws of the Union shall be faithfully executed in all the States. Doing this, which I deem to be only a simple duty on my part, I shall perfectly perform it, so far as is practicable, unless my rightful masters, the American people, shall withhold the requisition, or in some authoritative manner direct the contrary.

"I trust this will not be regarded as a menace, but only as the declared purpose of the Union that it will constitutionally defend and maintain itself.

"In doing this there need be no bloodshed or violence; and there shall be none unless it is forced upon the national authority.

WHAT SHALL BE DONE?

"The power confided to me will be used to hold, occupy, and possess the property and places belonging to the Government, and collect the duties and imposts; but beyond what may be necessary for these objects, there will be no invasion, no using of force against or among the people anywhere.

"Where hostility to the United States shall be so great and so universal as to prevent the competent resident citizens from holding federal offices, there will be no attempt to force obnoxious strangers among the people that object. While the strict legal right may exist in the Government to enforce the exercise of these offices, the attempt to do so would be so irritating, and so nearly impracticable withal, that I deem it best to forego, for the time, the uses of such offices.

"The mails, unless repelled, will continue to be furnished in all parts of the Union.

"So far as possible, the people everywhere shall have that sense of perfect security which is most favorable to calm thought and reflection.

"The course here indicated will be followed, unless current events and experience shall show a modification or change to be proper; and in every case and exigency my best discretion will be exercised according to the circumstances actually existing, and with a view and hope of a peaceable solution of the national troubles, and the restoration of fraternal sympathies and affections.

"That there are persons in one section or another who seek to destroy the Union at all events, and are glad of any pretext to do it, I will neither affirm nor deny. But if there be such, I need address no word to them.

A WORD TO THOSE WHO LOVE THE UNION

"To those, however, who love the Union, may I not speak, before entering upon so grave a matter as the destruction of our national fabric, with all its benefits, its memories and its hopes? Would it not be well to ascertain why we do it? Will you hazard so desperate a step, while there is any possibility that any portion of the ills you fly from have no real existence? Will you, while the certain ills you fly to are greater than all the real ones you fly from—will you risk the commission of so fearful a mistake? All profess to be content in the Union, if all Constitutional rights can be maintained. Is it true, then, that any right, plainly written in the Constitution, has been denied? I think not. Happily the human mind is so constituted that no party can reach to the audacity of doing this.

"Think, if you can, of a single instance in which a plainly-written provision of the Constitution has ever been denied. If, by the mere force of numbers, a majority should deprive a minority of any clearly-written Constitutional right, it might, in a moral point of view, justify revolution; it certainly would, if such a right were a vital one. But such is not our case.

"All the vital rights of minorities and of individuals are so plainly assured to them by affirmations and negations, guarantees and prohibitions in the Constitution, that controversies never arise concerning them. But no organic law can ever be framed with provisions specifically applicable to every question which may occur in practical administration. No foresight can anticipate, nor any document of reasonable length contain, express provisions for all possible questions. Shall fugitives from labor be surrendered by national or by State authorities? The Constitution does not expressly say. Must Congress protect slavery in the territories? The Constitution does not expressly say. From questions of this class spring all our Constitutional controversies, and we divide upon them into majorities and minorities.

THE MAJORITIES VS. THE MINORITIES

"If the minority did not acquiesce, the majority must, or the Government must cease. There is no alternative for continuing the Government acquiescence on the one side or the other. If a minority in such a case will secede rather than acquiesce, they make a precedent, which, in time, will ruin and divide them, for a minority of their own will secede from them whenever a majority refuses to be controlled by such a minority. For instance, why may not any portion of a new confederacy a year or two hence arbitrarily secede again, precisely as portions of the present Union now claim to secede from it? All who cherish disunion sentiments are now being educated to the exact temper of doing this. Is there such a perfect identity of interests among the States to compose a new Union as to produce harmony only, and prevent renewed secession? Plainly, the central idea of secession is the essence of anarchy.

"A majority held in check by Constitutional check limitation, and always changing easily with deliberate changes of popular opinions and sentiments, is the only true sovereign of a free people. Whoever rejects it does, of necessity, fly to anarchy or despotism. Unanimity is impossible; the rule of a minority, as a permanent arrangement, is wholly inadmissible. So that, rejecting the majority principle, anarchy or despotism, in some form, is all that is left.

"I do not forget the position assumed by some, that Constitutional questions are to be decided by the Supreme Court, nor do I deny that such decisions must be binding in any case upon the parties to a suit, while they are also entitled to a very high respect and consideration in all parallel cases by all the other departments of the Government; and while it is obviously possible that such a decision may be erroneous in any given case, still the evil following it, being limited to that particular case, with the chance that it may be overruled, and never become a precedent for other cases, can better be borne than could the evils of a different practice.

"At the same time, the candid citizen must confess that, if the policy of the Government upon the vital questions affecting the whole people is to be irrevocably fixed by the decisions of the Supreme Court the instant they are made, as in ordinary litigation between parties in personal action, the people will have ceased to be their own masters, unless having to that extent practically resigned their Government into the hands of that eminent tribunal.

"Nor is there in this view any assault upon the court or the judges. It is a duty from which they may not shrink, to decide cases properly brought before them; and it is no fault of theirs if others seek to turn their decisions to political purposes. One section of our country believes slavery is right, and ought to be extended, while the other believes that it is wrong, and ought not to be extended; and this is the only substantial dispute; and the fugitive slave clause of the Constitution and the law for the suppression of the slave trade are each as well enforced, perhaps, as any law can ever be in a community where the moral sense of the people imperfectly supports the law itself. The great body of the people abide by the dry legal obligation in both cases, and a few break over in each. This, I think, cannot be perfectly cured, and it would be worse, in both cases, after the separation of the sections than before. The foreign slave trade, now imperfectly suppressed, would be ultimately revived, without restriction in one section; while fugitive slaves, now only partially surrendered, would not be surrendered at all by the other.

WE CANNOT SEPARATE

"Physically speaking, we cannot separate; we cannot remove our respective sections from each other, nor build an impassable wall between them. A husband and wife may be divorced, and go out of the presence and beyond the reach of each other, but the different parts of our country cannot do this. They can but remain face to face, and intercourse, either amicable or hostile, must continue between them. Is it possible, then, to make that intercourse more advantageous or more satisfactory after separation than before? Can aliens make treaties easier than friends can make laws? Can treaties be more faithfully enforced between aliens than laws can among friends? Suppose you go to war, you cannot fight always; and when, after much loss on both sides, and no gain on either, you cease fighting, the identical questions as to terms of intercourse are again upon you.

THE PEOPLE

"This country, with its institutions, belongs to the people who inhabit it. Whenever they shall grow weary of the existing government, they can exercise their constitutional right of amending, or their revolutionary right to dismember or overthrow it. I cannot be ignorant of the fact that many worthy and patriotic citizens are desirous of having the national Constitution amended. While I make no recommendation of amendment, I fully recognize the full authority of the people over the whole subject, to be exercised in either of the modes prescribed in the instrument itself, and I should, under existing circumstances, favor rather than oppose, a fair opportunity being afforded the people to act upon it.

I will venture to add, that to me the convention mode seems preferable, in that it allows amendments to originate with the people themselves, instead of only permitting them to take or reject propositions originated by others not especially chosen for the purpose, and which might not be precisely such as they would wish either to accept or refuse. I understand that a proposed amendment to the Constitution (which amendment, however, I have not seen) has passed Congress, to the effect that the Federal Government shall never interfere with the domestic institutions of States, including that of persons held to service. To avoid misconstruction of what I have said, I depart from my purpose not to speak of particular amendments, so far as to say, that, holding such a provision now to be implied Constitutional law, I have no objections to its being made express and irrevocable.

THE ULTIMATE JUSTICE OF THE PEOPLE

"The chief magistrate derives all his authority from the people, and they have conferred none upon him to fix the terms for the separation of the States. The people, themselves, also, can do this if they choose; but the Executive, as such, has nothing to do with it. His duty is to administer the present Government as it came to his hands, and to transmit it unimpaired by him to his successor. Why should there not be a patient confidence in the ultimate justice of the people? Is there any better or equal hope in the world? In our present differences is either party without faith of being in the right? If the Almighty Ruler of nations, with His eternal truth and justice, be on your side of the North, or on yours of the South, that truth and that justice will surely prevail by the judgment of this great tribunal, the American people. By the frame of the Government under which we live, this same people have wisely given their public servants but little power for mischief, and have with equal wisdom provided for the return of that little to their own hands at very short intervals. While the people retain their virtue and vigilance, no administration, by any extreme wickedness or folly, can very seriously injure the Government in the short space of four years.

MY COUNTRYMEN, ONE AND ALL

"My countrymen, one and all, think calmly and well upon this subject. Nothing valuable can be lost by taking time.

"If there be an object to hurry any of you, in hot haste, to a step which you would never deliberately, that object will be frustrated by taking time; but no good can be frustrated by it.

"Such of you as are now dissatisfied still have the old Constitution unimpaired, and, on the sensitive point, the laws of your own framing under it; while the new administration will have no immediate power, if it would, to change either.

"If it were admitted that you who are dissatisfied hold the right side in the dispute, there is still no single reason for precipitate action. Intelligence, patriotism, Christianity, and a firm reliance upon Him who has never yet forsaken this favored land, are still competent to adjust, in the best way, all our present difficulty.

"In your hands, my dissatisfied fellow-countrymen, and not in mine, is the momentous issue of civil war. The Government will not assail you.

"You can have no conflict without being yourselves the aggressors. You have no oath registered in heaven to destroy the Government; while I shall have the most solemn one to preserve, protect and defend it.

"I am loth to close. We are not enemies, but friends. We must not be enemies. Though passion may have strained, it must not break our bonds of affection.

"The mystic cords of memory, stretching from every battle-field and patriot grave to every living heart and hearthstone all over this broad land, will yet swell the chorus of the Union, when again touched, as surely they will be, by the better angels of our nature."

REPLY TO THE COMMITTEE FROM THE VIRGINIA CONVENTION, APRIL 20, 1861

"To Hon. Messrs. Preston, Stuart, and Randolph.—Gentlemen: As a Committee of the Virginia Convention, now in session, you present me a preamble and resolution in these words:

" 'Whereas, In the opinion of this Convention, the uncertainty which prevails in the public mind as to the policy which the Federal Executive intends to pursue towards the seceded States, is extremely injurious to the industrial and commercial interests of the country, as it tends to keep up an excitement which is unfavorable to the adjustment of the pending difficulties, and threatens a disturbance of the public peace: Therefore, Resolved, That a committee of three delegates be appointed to wait on the President of the United States, present to him this preamble, and respectfully ask him to communicate to this Convention the policy which the Federal Executive intends to pursue in regard to the Confederate States.'

"In answer, I have to say that, having, at the beginning of my official term, expressed my intended policy as plainly as I was able, it is with deep regret and mortification I now learn there is great and injurious uncertainty in the public mind as to what the policy is, and what course I intend to pursue.

"Not having as yet seen occasion to change, it is now my purpose to pursue the course marked out in the Inaugural Address. I commend a careful consideration of the whole document as the best expression I can give to my purposes.

"As I then and therein said, I now repeat, the power confided in me will be used to hold, occupy and possess property and places belonging to the Government, and to collect the duties and imposts; but beyond what is necessary for these objects, there will be no invasion, no using of force against or among the people anywhere.

"By the words property and places belonging to the Government, I chiefly allude to the military posts and property which were in possession of the Government when it came into my hands. But if, as now appears to be true, in pursuit of a purpose to drive the United States authority from those places, an unprovoked assault has been made upon Fort Sumter, I shall hold myself at liberty to repossess it if I can, like places which had been seized before the Government was devolved upon me, and in any event I shall, to the best of my ability, repel force by force. In case it proves true that Fort Sumter has been assaulted as is reported, I shall, perhaps, cause the United States mails to be withdrawn from all the States which claim to have seceded, believing that commencement of actual war against the Government justifies and possibly demands it. I scarcely need to say that I consider the military posts and property situated within the States which claim to have seceded, as yet belonging to the Government of the United States as much as they did before the supposed secession.

"Whatever else I may do for the purpose, I shall not attempt to collect the duties and imposts by any armed invasion of any part of the country; not meaning by this, however, that I may not land a force deemed necessary to relieve a fort upon the border of the country. From the fact that I have quoted a part of the Inaugural Address, it must not be inferred that I repudiate any other part, the whole of which I re-affirm, except so far as what I now say of the mails may be regarded as a modification."

PROCLAMATION BY THE PRESIDENT

Washington, August 16, 1861.

By the President of the United States of America.

A PROCLAMATION

Whereas, on the fifteenth day of April, the President of the United States, in view of an insurrection against the laws, Constitution, and the Government of the United States, which had broken out within the States of South Carolina, Georgia, Alabama, Florida, Mississippi, Louisiana, and Texas, and in pursuance of the provision of the act entitled an act to provide for calling forth the militia to execute the laws of the Union, suppress insurrections and repel invasions, and to repeal the act now in force for that purpose, approved February 28, 1795, did call forth the militia to suppress said insurrection and cause the laws of the Union to be duly executed, and the insurgents have failed to disperse by the time directed by the President; and whereas such insurrection has since broken out and yet exists within the States of Virginia, North Carolina, Tennessee, and Arkansas; and whereas the insurgents in all the said States claim to act under authority thereof, and such claim is not disclaimed or repudiated by the person exercising the functions of government, in such States or in the part or parts thereof, in which combinations exist, nor has such insurrection been suppressed by said States. Now, therefore, I, Abraham Lincoln, President of the United States, in pursuance of an act of Congress, passed July 18, 1861, do hereby declare that the inhabitants of the said States of Georgia, South Carolina, Virginia, North Carolina, Tennessee, Alabama, Louisiana, Texas, Arkansas, Mississippi, and Florida (except the inhabitants of that part of Virginia lying west of the Alleghany Mountains, and of such other parts of that State, and the other States herein before named, as may maintain a loyal adhesion to the Union and the Constitution, or may be from time to time occupied and controlled by the forces engaged in the dispersion of said insurgents) are in a state of insurrection against the United States, and that all commercial intercourse between the same and the inhabitants thereof, with the exceptions aforesaid, and the citizens of other States and other parts of the United States is unlawful and will remain unlawful until such insurrection shall cease or has been suppressed; that all goods and chattels, wares and merchandise coming from any of said States, with the exceptions aforesaid, unto other parts of the United States, without the special license and permission of the President through the Secretary of the Treasury, or proceeding to any of said States, with the exceptions aforesaid, by land or water, together with the vessel or vehicle carrying the same, or conveying persons to or from said States, with said exceptions, will be forfeited to the United States, and that from and after fifteen days from the issuing of this proclamation, all ships and vessels belonging in whole or in part to any citizen or inhabitant of any of said States, with said exceptions, found at sea or in any port of the United States, will be forfeited to the United States, and I hereby enjoin upon all District Attorneys, Marshals, and officers of the revenue, and of the military and naval forces of the United States, to be vigilant in the execution of said act, and in the enforcement of the penalties and forfeitures imposed or declared by it, leaving any party who may think himself aggrieved thereby to his application to the Secretary of the Treasury, for the remission of any penalty or for forfeiture, which the said Secretary is authorized by law to grant, if, in his judgment, the special circumstances of any case shall require such remission.

In witness whereof, I have hereunto set my hand, and caused the seal of the United States to be affixed.

Done in the city of Washington, this 16th day of August, in the year of our Lord 1861, and of the Independence of the United States the eighty-sixth.

ABRAHAM LINCOLN.

By the President.
WM. H. SEWARD, Secretary of State.

THE EMANCIPATION QUESTION IN MISSOURI

The following is a letter from the President to General Fremont:

Washington, D. C., Sept. 11, 1861.

Maj.-Gen. John C. Fremont.

Sir: Yours of the 8th instant, in answer to mine of the 2d instant, was just received. Assured that you, upon the ground, could better judge of the necessities of your position, than I could at this distance, on seeing your proclamation of August 30th, I perceived no general objection to it; the particular clause, however, in relation to the confiscation of property and the liberation of slaves appeared to me objectionable in its non-conformity to the act of Congress, passed the 6th of last August, upon the same subjects, and hence I wrote you expressing my wish that that clause should be modified accordingly. Your answer just received expresses the preference on your part that I should make an open order for the modification, which I very cheerfully do. It is, therefore, ordered that the said clause of said proclamation be so modified, held, and construed as to conform with, and not to transcend, the provisions on the same subject contained in the act of Congress entitled, "An Act to confiscate property used for insurrectionary purposes," approved August 6, 1861, and that said Act be published at length with this order.

Your obedient servant,

A. Lincoln.

A PROCLAMATION

By the President of the United States of America.

In pursuance of the sixth section of the act of Congress entitled, "An Act to Suppress Insurrection, to Punish Treason and Rebellion, to Seize and Confiscate the Property of Rebels, and for other purposes," approved July 17, 1862, and which act and the joint resolution explanatory therein, are herewith published, I, Abraham Lincoln, President of the United States, do hereby proclaim to, and warn all persons within the contemplation of said sixth section, to cease participating in, aiding, countenancing, or abetting the existing rebellion, or any rebellion against the Government of the United States, and to return to their allegiance to the United States, on pain of the forfeitures and seizures as within and by said sixth section provided.

In testimony whereof, I have hereunto set my hand and caused the seal of the United States to be affixed.

Done at the city of Washington, this 25th day of July, in the year of our Lord one thousand eight hundred and sixty-two, and of the Independence of the United States the eighty-seventh.

By the President. A. LINCOLN.

WM. H. SEWARD, Secretary of State.

EXTRACTS UPON WHICH SEWARD BASED HIS "IRREPRESSIBLE-CONFLICT PLATFORM"

"In my opinion, it [the slavery agitation] will not cease until a crisis shall have been reached and passed.

"A house divided against itself cannot stand."

"I believe the government cannot remain permanently half slave and half free. I do not expect the Union to be dissolved—I do not expect the house to fall—but I do expect it will cease to be divided. It will become all one thing, or all the other. Either the opponents of slavery will arrest the further spread of it, and place it where the public mind shall rest in the belief that it is in the course of ultimate extinction; or its advocates will push it forward, till it shall become alike lawful in all the States, old as well as new—North as well as South."

"I have always hated slavery, I think, as much as any Abolitionist. I have been an old-line Whig. I have always hated it, and I always believed it in the course of ultimate extinction.

"If I were in Congress and a vote should come up whether slavery should be prohibited in a new Territory, in spite of the Dred Scott decision, I would vote that it should."

"I nevertheless did not mean to go to the banks of the Ohio and throw missiles into Kentucky, to disturb them in their domestic institutions.

"I believe that the right of property in a slave is not distinctly and expressly affirmed in the Constitution."

A PROCLAMATION

By the President of the United States of America:

Whereas, It has become necessary to call into service, not only volunteers, but also portions of the military of the States by draft, in order to suppress the insurrection existing in the United States, and disloyal persons are not adequately restrained by the ordinary processes of law from hindering these measures, and from giving aid and comfort in various ways to the insurrection, and as a necessary measure for suppressing the same, all rebels and insurgents, their aiders and abettors within the United States, and all persons discouraging volunteer enlistments, resisting military drafts, or guilty of any disloyal practice affording aid and comfort to the rebels against the authority of the United States, shall be subject to martial law, and liable to trial and punishment by courts-martial or military commission.

Second, That the writ of habeas corpus is suspended in respect to all persons arrested, or who are now, or hereafter, during the rebellion, shall be, imprisoned in any fort, camp, arsenal, military prison, or other places of confinement, or by the sentence of any court-martial or military commission.

In witness whereof I have hereunto set my hand, and caused the seal of the United States to be affixed.

Done at the city of Washington, this twenty-fourth day of September, in the year of our Lord one thousand eight hundred and sixty-two, and of the Independence of the United States the eighty-seventh.

By the President. ABRAHAM LINCOLN.
WM. H. SEWARD, Secretary of State.

A PROCLAMATION

On the sixth day of March last, by a special message, I recommended to Congress the adoption of a joint resolution, to be substantially as follows:

"Resolved, That the United States ought to co-operate with any State which may adopt a gradual abolishment of slavery, giving to such a State, in its discretion, compensation for the inconvenience, public and private, provided by such change of system."

The resolution, in the language above quoted, was adopted by large majorities in both branches of Congress, and now stands in authentic, definite, and solemn proposal of the nation to the States and people most immediately interested in the subject matter.

To the people of the States I now most earnestly appeal.

I do not argue, I beseech you to make the argument for yourselves.

You cannot, if you would, be blind to the signs of the times. I beg of you a calm and enlarged consideration of their import, ranging, if it may be, far above personal and partisan politics.

This proposal makes common cause for a common object, casting no reproaches upon any.

It acts not the Pharisee. The change it contemplates would come gently as the dews of heaven, not rending or wrecking anything.

Will you not embrace it? So much good has not been done by one effort in all past times, as in the Providence of God it is now your high privilege to do. May the vast future not have to lament that you have rejected it.

By the President. ABRAHAM LINCOLN.

WM. H. SEWARD, Secretary of State.

May 19, 1862.

EMANCIPATION PROCLAMATION

Issued by President Lincoln, January 1, 1863, at Washington

Whereas, on the twenty-second day of September, in the year of our Lord one thousand eight hundred and sixty-two, a proclamation was issued by the President of the United States, containing among other things, the following, to wit:

"That on the first day of January, in the year of our Lord one thousand eight hundred and sixty-three, all persons held as slaves within any State or designated part of a State, the people whereof shall then be in rebellion against the United States, shall be then, thenceforward, and forever free, and the Executive Government of the United States, including the military and naval authority thereof, will recognize and maintain the freedom of such persons, and will do no act or acts to repress such persons, or any of them, in any efforts they may make for their actual freedom.

"That the Executive will, on the first day of January aforesaid, by proclamation, designate the States and parts of States, if any, in which the people thereof respectively shall then be in rebellion against the United States; and the fact that any State or the people thereof shall on that day be in good faith represented in the Congress of the United States, by members chosen thereto, at elections wherein a majority of the qualified voters of such State shall have participated, shall, in the absence of a strong countervailing testimony, be deemed conclusive evidence that such State, and the people thereof, are not then in rebellion against the United States."

Now, therefore, I, Abraham Lincoln, President of the United States, by virtue of the power in me vested as Commander-in-Chief of the Army and Navy of the United States in time of actual armed rebellion against the authority and Government of the United States, and as a fit and necessary war measure for suppressing said rebellion, do, on the first day of January, in the year of our Lord one thousand eight hundred and sixty-three, and in accordance with my purpose so to do, publicly proclaimed for the full period of one hundred days from the day first above mentioned, order and designate, as the States and parts of States wherein the people thereof respectively are this day in rebellion against the United States, the following, to-wit:

Arkansas, Texas, Louisiana (except the parishes of St. Bernard, Plaquemine, Jefferson, St. John, St. Charles, St. James, Ascension, Assumption, Terre Bonne, Lafourche, St. Marie, St. Martin, and Orleans, including the City of New Orleans), Mississippi, Alabama, Florida, Georgia, North Carolina, South Carolina and Virginia (except the forty-eight counties designated as West Virginia, and also the counties of Berkeley, Accomac, Northampton, Elizabeth City, York, Princess Anne, and Norfolk, including the cities of Norfolk and Portsmouth), and which excepted parts are for the present left precisely as if this proclamation were not issued.

And, by virtue of the power and for the purpose aforesaid, I do order and declare that all persons held as slaves within said designated States and parts of States, are, and henceforward shall be, free; and that the Executive Government of the United States, including the military and naval authorities thereof, will recognize and maintain the freedom of said persons.

And I hereby enjoin upon the people so declared to be free, to abstain from all violence, unless in necessary self-defense; and I recommend to them, that in all cases, when allowed, they labor faithfully for reasonable wages.

And I further declare and make known that such persons of suitable condition will be received into the armed service of the United States, to garrison forts, positions, stations and other places, and to man vessels of all sorts in said service.

And upon this act, sincerely believed to be an act of justice, warranted by the Constitution, upon military necessity, I invoke the considerate judgment of mankind, and the gracious favor of the Almighty God.

In testimony whereof, I have hereunto set my name, and caused the seal of the United States to be affixed.

[L. S.] Done at the City of Washington, this first day of January, in the year of our Lord one thousand eight hundred and sixty-three, and of the Independence of the United States the eighty-seventh.

By the President. ABRAHAM LINCOLN.
WILLIAM H. SEWARD, Secretary of State.

LINCOLN'S SPEECH AT GETTYSBURG

Delivered at the dedication of the Gettysburg National Cemetery on the Gettysburg battlefield, November 19, 1863:

"Ladies and Gentlemen: Fourscore and seven years ago our fathers brought forth upon this continent a new nation, conceived in liberty, and dedicated to the proposition that all men are created equal. Now we are engaged in a great civil war, testing whether that nation, or any nation so conceived and so dedicated, can long endure. We are met on a great battlefield of that war. We have come to dedicate a portion of that field as a final resting-place for those who here gave their lives that that nation might live. It is altogether fitting and proper that we should do this.

"But in a larger sense, we cannot dedicate, we cannot consecrate, we cannot hallow, this ground. The brave men, living and dead, who struggled here, have consecrated it far above our power to add or detract. The world will little note, nor long remember, what we say here; but it can never forget what they did here.

"It is for us, the living, rather to be dedicated here to the unfinished work which they who fought here have thus far so nobly advanced. It is rather for us to be here dedicated to the great task remaining before us, that from these honored dead we take increased devotion to that cause for which they gave the last full measure of devotion; that we here highly resolve that these dead shall not have died in vain; that this nation, under God, shall have a new birth of freedom, and that government of the people, by the people, for the people, shall not perish from the earth."

THE RIGHTS OF LABOR (EXTRACT), APRIL, 1864

"To New York Workmen's Association: The most notable feature of the disturbance in your city last summer was the hanging of some working people by other working people.

"It should never be so. The strongest bond of human

sympathy outside of the family relation should be one uniting all working people of all nations, tongues, and kindreds, nor should this lead to a war on property or owners of property.

"Property is the fruit of labor. Property is desirable—is a positive good in the world. That some should be rich shows that others may become rich, and hence is just encouragement to industry and enterprise. Let not him who is houseless pull down the house of another, but let him labor diligently and build one for himself, thus by example assuring himself that his own shall be safe from violence when built."

RESPONSE TO SERENADE FROM MARYLANDERS, WASHINGTON, NOVEMBER, 1864

"I am notified that this is a compliment paid me by the loyal Marylanders resident in this district.

"I infer that the adoption of the new Constitution for the State furnishes the occasion; and that in your view the extirpation of slavery constitutes the chief merit of the new Constitution.

"Most heartily do I congratulate you and Maryland, and the nation, and the world, upon the event. I regret that it did not occur two years sooner, which, I am sure, would have saved the nation more money than would have met all the private loss incident to the measure; but it has come at last, and I sincerely hope its friends may realize all their anticipations of good from it, and that its opponents may, by its effect, be agreeably and profitably disappointed. A word upon another subject:

"Something said by the Secretary of State in his recent

speech at Auburn has been construed by some into a threat that, if I shall be beaten at the election, I will, between then and the end of my Constitutional term, do what I may be able to ruin the Government.

"Others regard the fact that the Chicago Convention adjourned, not sine die, but to meet again, if called to do so, by a particular individual, as the ultimatum of a purpose that if the nominee shall be elected he will at once seize control of the Government. I hope the good people will not allow themselves to suffer any uneasiness on either point. I am struggling to maintain the Government, not to overthrow it. I therefore say that, if I shall live, I shall remain President until the 4th of next March. And whoever shall be constitutionally elected therefor in November, shall be duly installed as President on the 4th of March, and that in the interval I shall do my utmost that whoever is to hold the helm for the next voyage shall start with the best possible chance to save the ship.

"This is due to the people, both in principle and under the Constitution. Their will, constitutionally expressed, is the ultimate law of all.

"If they should deliberately resolve to have immediate peace, even at the loss of their country, and their liberties, I know not the power or the right to resist them.

"It is their own business, and they must do as they please with their own. I believe, however, they are all resolved to preserve their country and their liberty; and in this, in office or out of it, I am resolved to stand by them. I may add, that in this purpose to save the country and its liberties, no class of people seem so nearly unanimous as the soldiers in the field and the seamen afloat. Do they not have the hardest of it? Who should quail when they do not? God bless the soldiers and seamen and all their brave commanders.

"ABRAHAM LINCOLN."

THE PRESIDENT TO LIEUTENANT-GENERAL GRANT

Executive Mansion, Washington, April 30, 1864.

Lieutenant-General Grant:

Not expecting to see you before the spring campaign opens, I wish to express in this way my entire satisfaction with what you have done up to this time, so far as I understand it.

The particulars of your plan I neither know, nor seek to know. You are vigilant and self-reliant, and, pleased with this, I wish not to obtrude any restraints or constraints upon you. While I am very anxious that any great disaster, or capture of our men in great numbers, shall be avoided, I know that these points are less likely to escape your attention than they would be mine. If there be anything wanting, which is within my power to give, do not fail to let me know it.

And now, with a brave army and a just cause, may God sustain you. Yours very truly,

ABRAHAM LINCOLN.

SECOND NOMINATION

Executive Mansion, Washington, June 27, 1864.

Hon. William Dennison and Others, a Committee of the National Union Convention.

Gentlemen: Your letter of the 14th instant, formally

notifying me that I have been nominated by the Convention you represent for the Presidency of the United States for four years from the 4th of March next, has been received. The nomination is gratefully accepted, as the Resolutions of the Convention—called the platform—are heartily approved.

While the resolution in regard to supplanting of Republican government upon the Western continent is fully concurred in, there might be some misunderstanding were I not to say that the position of the Government in relation to the action of France in Mexico, as assumed through the State Department and endorsed by the Convention, among the measures and acts of the Executive, will be faithfully maintained so long as the state of facts shall leave that position permanent and applicable.

I am especially gratified that the soldier and the seaman were not forgotten by the Convention, as they forever must and will be remembered by the grateful country for whose salvation they devoted their lives.

Thanking you for the kind and complimentary terms in which you have communicated the nomination and other proceedings of the Convention, I subscribe myself,

Your obedient servant,

ABRAHAM LINCOLN.

LINCOLN'S SECOND INAUGURAL

Delivered March 4, 1865, at Washington.

WITH MALICE TOWARDS NONE, WITH CHARITY FOR ALL

"Fellow-Countrymen: At this second appearing to take the oath of the Presidential office, there is less occasion for an extended address than there was at the first.

Then, a statement somewhat in detail of a course to be pursued seemed very fitting and proper. Now, at the expiration of four years, during which public declarations have been constantly called forth on every point and phase of the great contest which still absorbs the attention and engrosses the energies of the nation, little that is new could be presented.

"The progress of our arms, upon which all else chiefly depends, is as well known to the public as to myself; and it is, I trust, reasonably satisfactory and encouraging to all. With high hope for the future, no prediction in regard to it is ventured.

"On the occasion corresponding to this four years ago, all thoughts were anxiously directed to an impending civil war. All dreaded it; all sought to avoid it. While the inaugural address was being delivered from this place, devoted altogether to save the Union without war, insurgent agents were in the city seeking to destroy it without war—seeking to dissolve the Union and divide the effects by negotiation. Both parties deprecated war; but one of them would make war rather than let the nation survive, and the other would accept war rather than let it perish; and the war came.

"One-eighth of the whole population were colored slaves, not distributed generally over the Union, but localized in the southern part of it. These slaves constituted a peculiar and powerful interest. All knew that this interest was somehow the cause of the war. To strengthen, perpetuate and extend this interest, was the object for which the insurgents would rend the Union even by war, while the Government claimed no right to do more than to restrict the territorial enlargement of it.

"Neither party expected for the war the magnitude or

the duration which it has already attained. Neither anticipated that the cause of the conflict might cease with, or even before, the conflict itself would cease. Each looked for an easier triumph, and a result less fundamental and astounding.

"Both read the same Bible and pray to the same God, and each invokes his aid against the other. It may seem strange that any man should dare to ask a just God's assistance in wringing their bread from the sweat of other men's faces; but let us judge not, that we be not judged. The prayers of both could not be answered. That of neither has been answered fully. The Almighty has His own purposes. 'Woe unto the world because of offenses, for it must needs be that offenses come; but woe to that man by whom the offense cometh.' If we shall suppose that American slavery is one of these offenses, which in the Providence of God must needs come, but which, having continued through His appointed time, He now wills to remove, and that He gives to both North and South this terrible war as the woe due to those by whom the offense came, shall we discern therein any departure from those divine attributes which the believers in a living God always ascribe to Him?

"Fondly do we hope, fervently do we pray, that this mighty scourge of war may soon pass away. Yet, if God wills that it continue until the wealth piled by the bondsman's two hundred and fifty years of unrequited toil shall be sunk, and until every drop of blood drawn by the lash shall be paid by another drawn with the sword, as was said three thousand years ago, so still it must be said, that 'the judgments of the Lord are true and righteous altogether.'

"With malice towards none, with charity for all, with

firmness in the right, as God gives us to see the right, let us finish the work we are in, to bind up the nation's wounds, to care for him who shall have borne the battle, and for his widow and orphans, to do all which may achieve and cherish a just and a lasting peace among ourselves and with all nations."

PRESIDENT LINCOLN'S LAST SPEECH

A carefully worded, wise and memorable production, delivered Tuesday evening, April 11, 1865, in response to a serenade at the White House:

"Fellow Citizens: We meet this evening not in sorrow, but in gladness of heart. The evacuation of Petersburg and Richmond, and the surrender of the principal insurgent army, give hope of a righteous and speedy peace whose joyous expression cannot be restrained. In the midst of this, however, He from whom all blessings flow must not be forgotten. A call for a national thanksgiving is being prepared, and will be duly promulgated. Nor must those whose harder part gives us the cause of rejoicing be overlooked. Their honors must not be parceled out with the others. I myself was near the front, and had the high pleasure of transmitting much of the good news to you; but no part of the honor, for plan or execution, is mine. To General Grant, his skillful officers and brave men, all belongs. The gallant navy stood ready, but was not in reach to take active part.

"By these recent successes, the re-inauguration of the national authority, reconstruction, which has had a large share of thought from the first, is pressed much more closely upon our attention. It is fraught with great difficulty. Unlike the case of a war between independent nations, there is no authorized organ for us to treat with. No man has authority to give up the rebellion for any other man. We simply must begin with and mold from disorganized and discordant elements. Nor is it a small additional embarrassment that we, the loyal people, differ among ourselves as to the mode, manner and means of reconstruction.

"As a general rule, I abstain from reading the reports of attacks upon myself, wishing not to be provoked by that to which I cannot properly offer an answer. In spite of this precaution, however, it comes to my knowledge that I am much censured from some supposed agency in setting up and seeking to sustain the new State Government of Louisiana. In this I have done just so much, and no more than, the public knows. In the annual message of December, 1863, and accompanying proclamation, I presented a plan of reconstruction (as the phrase goes) which I promised, if adopted by any State, should be acceptable to, and sustained by, the Executive Government of the nation. I distinctly stated that this was not the only plan which might possibly be acceptable; and I also distinctly protested that the Executive claimed no right to say when or whether members should be admitted to seats in Congress from such States. This plan was, in advance, submitted to the then Cabinet, and distinctly approved by every member of it. One of them suggested that I should then, and in that connection, apply the Emancipation Proclamation to the heretofore excepted parts of Virginia and Louisiana; that I should drop the suggestion about apprenticeship for freed people, and that I should omit the protest against my own power, in regard to the admission of members of Congress, but even he approved every part and parcel of the plan which has since been employed or touched by the actions of Louisiana.

"The new Constitution of Louisiana, declaring emancipation for the whole State, practically applies the proclamation to the part previously excepted. It does not adopt apprenticeship to freed people, and it is silent, as it could not well be otherwise, about the admission of members of Congress. So that, as it applies to Louisiana, every member of the Cabinet fully approved the plan. The message went to Congress, and I received many commendations of the plan, written and verbal; and not a single objection to it, from any professed emancipationist, came to my knowledge, until after the news reached Washington that the people of Louisiana had begun to move in accordance with it. From about July, 1862, I had corresponded with different persons supposed to be interested, seeking a reconstruction of a State Government for Louisiana. When the message of 1863, with the plan before mentioned, reached New Orleans, General Banks wrote me he was confident that the people, with his military cooperation, would reconstruct substantially on that plan. I wrote him, and some of them, to try it. They tried it, and the result is known. Such only has been my agency in getting up the Louisiana Government. As to sustaining it, my promise is out, as before stated.

"But, as bad promises are better broken than kept, I shall treat this as a bad promise, and break it, whenever I shall be convinced that keeping it is adverse to the public interest. But I have not yet been so convinced.

"I have been shown a letter on this subject, supposed to be an able one, in which the writer expresses regret that my mind has not seemed to be definitely fixed on the question whether the seceded States, so called, are in the Union or out of it. It would, perhaps, add astonishment to his regret to learn that, since I have found professed Union men endeavoring to make that question, I have purposely forborne any public expression upon it. As appears to me, that question has not been, nor yet is, a practically material one, and that any discussion of it, while it thus remains practically immaterial, could have no effect other than the mischievous one of dividing our friends.

"As yet, whatever it may hereafter become, that question is bad, as the basis of a controversy, and good for nothing at all—a merely pernicious abstraction. We all agree that the seceded States, so called, are out of their proper relation to the Union, and that the sole object of the Government, civil and military, in regard to those States, is to again get them into their proper practical relation. I believe it is not only possible, but, in fact, easier to do this without deciding, or even considering, whether these States have ever been out of the Union, than with it. Finding themselves safely at home, it would be utterly immaterial whether they had ever been abroad. Let us all join in doing the acts necessary to restoring the proper practical relations between these States and the Union, and each forever after innocently indulge his own opinion whether, in doing the acts, he brought the States from without into the Union, or only gave them proper assistance, they never having been out of it.

"The amount of constituency, so to speak, on which the new Louisiana Government rests would be more satisfactory to all if it contained fifty, thirty, or even twenty thousand, as it really does. It is also unsatisfactory to some that the election franchise is not given to the colored man. I would myself prefer that it were now conferred on the very intelligent and those who serve our cause as soldiers. Still, the question is not whether the Louisiana Government, as it stands, is quite all that is desirable. The question is, 'Will it be wiser to take it as it is, or to reject and disperse it?'

"Can Louisiana be brought into proper practical relation with the Union sooner by sustaining or discarding the new State Government?

"Some twelve thousand voters in the heretofore Slave State of Louisiana have sworn allegiance to the Union, assumed to be the rightful political power of the State, held elections, organized a State Government, adopted a Free State constitution, giving the benefit of public schools equally to black and white, and empowering the Legislature to confer elective franchise upon the colored man. The Legislature has already voted to ratify the Constitutional amendment passed by Congress, abolishing slavery throughout the nation. These twelve thousand persons are thus fully committed to the Union and to perpetual freedom in the States—committed to the very things, and nearly all the things, the nation wants—and they ask the nation's recognition and its assistance to make good that committal.

"Now, if we reject and spurn them, we do our utmost to disorganize and disperse them. We, in effect, say to the white men: 'You are worthless, or worse; we will neither help you, nor be helped by you.' To the blacks we say: 'This cup of liberty which these, your old masters, hold to your lips, we will dash from you, and leave you to the chances of gathering the spilled and scattered contents in some vague and undefined when, where and how.' If this course, discouraging and paralyzing both white and black, has any tendency to bring Louisiana into proper practical relations with the Union, I have, so far, been unable to perceive it. If, on the contrary, we recognize and sustain the new government of Louisiana, the converse of all this is made true.

"We encourage the hearts and nerve the arms of the twelve thousand to adhere to their work, and argue for it, and proselyte for it, fight for it, and feed it, and grow it and ripen it to a complete success. The colored man, too, seeing all united for him, is inspired with vigilance, and energy, and daring the same end. Grant that he desires elective franchise, will he not obtain it sooner by saving the already advanced steps towards it, than by running backward over them? Concede that the new government of Louisiana is only as to what it should be as the egg is to the fowl, we shall sooner have the fowl by hatching the egg than by smashing it. [Laughter.]

"Again, if we reject Louisiana, we also reject one vote in favor of the proposed amendment to the National Constitution. To meet this proposition, it has been argued that no more than three-fourths of those States which have not attempted secession are necessary to validly ratify the amendment. I do not commit myself against this, further than to say that such a ratification would be questionable, and sure to be persistently questioned, while ratification by three-fourths of all the States would be unquestioned and unquestionable.

"I repeat the question: 'Can Louisiana be brought into proper practical relation with the Union sooner by sustaining or by discarding her new State Government?' What has been said of Louisiana will apply generally to other States. And yet so great peculiarities pertain to each State, and such important and sudden changes occur in the same State, and, withal, so new and unprecedented is the whole case, that no exclusive and inflexible plan can safely be prescribed as to details and collaterals. Such exclusive and inflexible plan would surely become a new entanglement. Important principles may, and must be, flexible.

"In the present situation, as the phrase goes, it may be my duty to make some new announcement to the people of the South. I am considering, and shall not fail to act, when satisfied that action will be proper."

PRESIDENT LINCOLN'S LETTER TO MRS. BIXBY

Executive Mansion, Nov. 21, 1864.

Dear Madam: I have been shown in the files of the War Department a statement of the Adjutant-General of Massachusetts that you are the mother of five sons who have died gloriously on the field of battle. I feel how weak and fruitless must be any words of mine which should attempt to beguile you from the grief of a loss so overwhelming. But I cannot refrain from tendering you the consolation that may be found in the thanks of the Republic they died to save. I pray that our Heavenly Father may assuage the anguish of your bereavement and leave you only the cherished memory of the loved and lost, and the solemn pride that must be yours to have laid so costly a sacrifice upon the altar of freedom.

Yours very sincerely and respectfully,

(Signed) ABRAHAM LINCOLN.